Homophobia
and the
Judaeo-Christian
Tradition

Gay Men's Issues in Religious Studies Series
Volume 1
American Academy of Religion

Essays by
J. Michael Clark
Gary David Comstock
Lewis John Eron
Mark R. Kowalewski
Bruce L. Mills
Craig Wesley Pilant
Michael L. Stemmeler
Thomas M. Thurston

Edited by
Michael L. Stemmeler &
J. Michael Clark

Dallas
Monument Press
1990

© 1990, Monument Press

Library of Congress Cataloging-in-Publication Data

Homophobia and the Judaeo-Christian tradition : essays / by
    J. Michael Clark . . . [et al.] : edited by Michael L.
    Stemmeler & J. Michael Clark.
    p.   cm. -- (Gay men's issues in religious studies series : v.
1)
    Essays originally presented at the Gay men's issues in
religion consultation during the 1988 annual convention of
the American Academy of Religion, held in Chicago.
    Includes bibliographical references and index.
    ISBN 0-930383-18-4 : $20.00
    1. Homosexuality--Religious aspects--Christianity--
Congresses. 2. Homosexuality--Religious aspects--Judaism--
Congresses. 3. Homosexuality--Biblical teaching--
Congresses. 4. Gay men--Religious life--Congresses. I. Clark,
J. Michael (John Michael), 1953-   . II. Stemmeler, Michael
L., 1955-   . III. Series.
BR115.H6H62 1990   90-46566
261.8'35766--dc20   CIP

Proudly published by Monument Press
Distributed by Publishers Associates
All rights reserved

Acknowledgements:

"Patriarchy, Dualism, and Homophobia: Marginalization as Spiritual Challenge," and " 'Coming Out'. Discovering Empowerment, Balance, and Wholeness," are excerpted from J. Michael Clark, *A Place to Start: Toward an Unapologetic Gay Liberation Theology*, © Monument Press, 1989. Used by permission.

"Theological and Ethical Implications of Homophobic Violence," is excerpted from Gary David Comstock, *Violence against Lesbians and Gay Men*, © Columbia University Press, 1990. Used by permission.

iii

FORTHCOMING

Gay Men's Issues in Religious Studies Series

Volume 2: Proceedings of the Gay Men's Issues in Religion Consultation, American Academy of Religion, Fall 1989, Anaheim:

Constructing Gay Theology
including papers by J. MIchael Clark, Michael Gorman, and Thomas M. Thurston, with a response by Father John J. McNeil, S.J.

Volume 3: Proceedings of the Gay Men's Issues in Religion Consultation, American Academy of Religion, Fall 1990, New Orleans:

Homosexuality and Non-Christian Religious Traditions
including papers by Gary David Comstock, Paul G. Schalow, and Giovanni Vitiello, with a response by José I. Cabezon.

Table of Contents

The Contemporary Situation

Conclusion: Beyond Homophobia through Coming Out

INTRODUCTION

On the Inaugeral Volume of the Gay Men's Issues in Religious Studies Series

There is a growing demand in the various disciplines of religious studies for a critical perspective on intellectual issues facing gay men. Published scholarship and theological reflection upon gay men and religion has existed for some time: no forum has existed, however, to facilitate the systematization, or to stem the fragmentation of, scholarship on these issues. The Gay Men's Issues in Religious Studies series will serve as an opportunity toward the symbiosis of religious and gay (male) studies.

We are happy to present to the reader the first volume of the Gay Men's Issues in Religious Studies series. The series intends to publish refereed, scholarly investigations into the vast field of the interrelations between religion in general and the world's religions, on the one hand, and the being, spirituality, and sexuality of gay men, on the other. It intends to be more than a narrowly focused religious studies series. Data and modes of analysis from a variety of scholarly disciplines, particularly the social sciences, will be introduced through the articles. History, law, and medicine occupy auxiliary positions. The focus of the series will be narrow, however, in that it does not want to be a general gay studies publication, as valuable as such publications are for religious studies scholars. At the heart of this and future volumes in the series is the cross-referential and interdisciplinary study of gay male issues and religion.

A word needs to be said about the genesis of the series. In the fall of 1987, the American Academy of Religion held its annual convention in Boston. Many gay men among the convention participants attended the program unit of the Lesbian-Feminist Issues in Religion Consultation and realized that a corresponding program unit of such high quality was not in existence for gay men at that time. The now Lesbian-Feminist Group of the AAR is to be commended for having facilitated the birthing process of the Gay Men's Issues in Religion Consultation which has now been accorded Group status within the AAR and which, as such, now enters its third year. The genesis of the gay men's group may serve as a most unconventional example of parthenogenesis.

After the approval of the formation of the Gay Men's Issues in Religion Consultation, by the Program Committee of the AAR in late 1987, paper proposals were solicited for the first session of the consultation in Chicago in 1988. The theme for the session was "Homophobia in Religion and Society: Its History and Effects." The broad phrasing of the theme generated a significant response from the AAR membership. The present volume features the papers which were actually presented in Chicago. In addition, it contains a number of papers addressing homophobia in the Judaeo-Christian tradition from perspectives not directly represented at the original program session. They contribute significantly, nevertheless, to the development of a more comprehensive picture of the origin(s) and the extent of homophobia in religion and society.

As the title of this volume suggests, the focal point of the contributions is the Judaeo-Christian tradition. There is a reason for this limitation and it is not to be understood as exclusive in meaning. The reason lies in the responses to the original call for papers; the theme of the first consultation invited responses from all types of religious and social experience and homosexuality. The papers, however, addressed exclusively problem areas in the Jewish and Christian traditions in the West. The anticipated third volume of this series, from the 1990 group meetings in New Orleans, will partly remedy this predicament; it will thematize gay religious experience in the various non-Christian traditions (volume two, from the 1989 consultation in Anaheim, will focus on methodologies for constructing gay theology).

The present volume is divided into three sections, largely along methodological lines: textual and historical analyses, social-scientific analyses, and psychological and pastoral interpretations. Past and present anathematizing of gay being and gay sexual activity drew their support from the scriptural sources of the Jewish and Christian traditions with their underlying affirmation of a patriarchal, and heterosexist, social structure. The initial textual and historical analyses ("Leviticus 18:22"; "The Testament of Naphtali"; "Patriarchy, Dualism and Homophobia") highlight paradigmatically the hermeneutical trajectories of homophobia in religion and society.

This section is followed by social-scientific analysis. The contribution on both Nazi and post-war German social and legal policies toward gays examines the effects of a racist and national-populist sexual morality in recent world history. Theological and ethical implications of contemporary homophobic violence are presented in the second paper in this section. The point developed from historical overview and empirical data is that the attacked form movements of solidarity in response to encountered violence. Therewith, greater visibility is achieved and the "strangers" are enabled to a more effective position within society.

The third section is devoted to a critique of the contemporary situation of homophobia in (organized) religion and society. The first article investigates word and meaning in ecclesiastical statements on human sexuality, sexual orientation, and genital activity. Next is a focus on the Janus-faced quality of the AIDS crisis. On the one hand, it can be utilized to legitimate homophobia and to assist in the generation of socially disruptive legislation which receives the blessing of the leaders of organized religion; on the other hand, the crisis can serve to amalgamate a grassroots militancy for change in religion and society. In that respect the AIDS crisis could be interpreted as a catalyst for change. The last paper in this

section explores the interconnection of homophobia and
AIDS from the psychoanalytical perspective. The ellipitical
poles of fear and passion serve as the backdrop against which
rationalizations of homophobia, as well as the dynamics of
homosexual attraction and revulsion, are projected.

Homophobia itself should not have the last word, however, particularly in a study whose ultimate goal is liberation.
A prospective contribution is therefore positioned as the conclusion of this volume. The discovery of socio-political empowerment, and of spiritual balance and psycho-physical
wholeness, points toward the work and the pleasures, the
tears of struggle and the tears of joy, which lie ahead.

—Michael L. Stemmeler, Ph.D.

5

TEXTUAL/HISTORICAL ANALYSES

"Past and present anathematizing of gay being and gay sexual activity drew their support from the scriptural sources of the Jewish and Christian traditions with their underlying affirmation of a patriarchal, and heterosexist, social structure. The initial textual and historical analyses, presented in this section ("Leviticus 18:22"; "The Testament of Naphtali"; "Patriarchy, Dualism and Homophobia"), highlight paradigmatically the hermeneutical trajectories of homophobia in religion and society."

Leviticus 18:22
and the Prohibition of Homosexual Acts

The levitical prohibition, *"You shall not lie with a male as with a woman; it is an abomination"* (Lev. 18:22 RSV) is the most significant passage in the Old Testament concerning homosexual acts. This passage, along with the corresponding punishment given in Leviticus 20:13, constitutes the only place in the Old Testament where homosexual acts are treated explicitly. Up until now, exegetes have not given the verse extended attention. Nevertheless, the passage has received considerable attention from those involved in the current debate on Christianity and homosexuality. The interest has come almost exclusively from those who wish Christian churches to take a more tolerant attitude toward homosexual relations. This paper will explore the use of Lev. 18:22 in this debate, then explore the original intent of the passage, and finally suggest how the passage should be used in Christian ethical discussion.

Lev. 18:22 in the Context of the Contemporary Debate on Homosexuality

D. S. Bailey opened the topic of homosexuality to theological reconsideration in the 1950s in his landmark book, *Homosexuality and the Western Christian Tradition.* Although his readings of biblical passages are generally sympathetic with the interests of homosexuals, Baily finds this passage an unambiguous condemnation of all homosexual acts.[1] Less sympathetic readers can find this passage's clear phrasing a convenient prooftext for justifying their intolerance of homosexual expression.

John McNeill, who has developed the most thorough argument for the morality of homosexual relations to date, gives a number of reasons for the levitical prohibition, but no sustained argument. The passage is from the section of Leviticus known as the Holiness Code. McNeill points out that generally the Code is directed against the idolatrous practices of the Canaanites, and this prohibition must be read in that light. Other cultural and historical circumstances include the pro-fertility bent of the Old Testament and the Hebrew stress on preserving the family name through progeny. McNeill points out that the act of sodomy was seen as an expression of domination, contempt and scorn, an attitude which is illustrated in the Sodom story (Gen. 19.1-29). He cites Walter Brun in reminding us that the main reason homosexual practices were thought abominable was that one man uses another as a woman, and the other allows himself to be used as a woman. Thus, both men dishonor the dignity of the male.[2] This reasoning explains the absence of any mention of female homosexual practices.

John Boswell, in reading Lev. 18:22, does not interpret in the labeling homosexual acts as an abomination (*toevah*) a reference to something intrinsically evil, like rape or theft. Rather, he sees *toevah* as referring to something which is ritually unclean, like eating pork or engaging in intercourse during menstruation. Boswell argues that *toevah* is associated particularly with the uncleanness of the Gentiles and with idolatry, by looking at the rest of Lev. 18. The chapter forms a unit which begins and ends with warnings against following the practices of other nations, particularly the Canaanites. Boswell finds in the foreignness of these practices the basis of their uncleanness. The verse immediately preceding the verse on homosexual acts refers to an idolatrous act: offering children to the god Molech. He concludes that the laws of Lev. 18, with their corresponding punishments in Lev. 20, are to be seen as symbols of Jewish distinctiveness.[3]

Boswell suggests a further problem. For both Jesus and Paul it was not the physical violation of Levitical precepts which constituted abomination, but the interior infidelity of the soul. To impose certain portions of Leviticus would have seemed prejudicial. The Levitical prohibition against same-sex behavior would have struck Roman citizens as to be as arbitrary as the prohibition of cutting the beard, and they would have paid no more attention to one than to the other.[4]

Boswell further notes that almost no early Christian writer appealed to Leviticus as an authority against homosexual acts. Even though a few did cite Leviticus, Boswell maintains that this passage cannot have been the origin of their attitude toward homosexual acts, since they rejected the vast majority of Levitical precepts.[5]

Boswell's multisided argument has numerous difficulties. However, he does raise two important issues: the question of the status of Lev. 18:22 as a ritual cleanliness regulation, and the question of the status of levitical law in the early Christian community. These and other issues Boswell raises will be addressed in greater detail later in this paper.

Since the Holiness Code dates to a period during or just after the Babylonian exile, Tom Horner, in his extended study on the Bible and homosexuality, attributes the prohibition of homosexual acts to Persian influence. No people in history were more opposed to homosexuality than they. Zoroastrian scriptures describe the devil as the man who lies with mankind as man lies with womankind. Such a man may be killed without any official authorization.[6]

Horner further claims that the Levitical prohibition must also be seen in the light of Deut. 23:17-18, the prohibition of male and female cult prostitutes, drawing the comparison to the Galli who served Cybele after castrating themselves.[7] He finds unconvincing efforts to show that the Galli functioned heterosexually.[8] The King James Version translates *kedesh* not as male cult prostitute but as sodomite, thus, in Horner's thinking, preserving the homosexual reference of the term. The abomination in Lev. 18:22, Horner claims, is the same as the abomination in Deut. 23:18.

A difficulty with Horner's twofold position—arguing the

Persian influence on the one hand and the concern about
male cult prostitution on the other—is that such a form of
idolatry was not a problem during the Persian period. A concern with idolatry must indicate an earlier origin of the passage. If Persian influence was a cause of the prohibition,
concern about *kedeshim* was not.

The difficulty in interpreting these passages is reinforced
by the fact, observed by Robin Scroggs, that no other passage
in the Old Testament refers to this Levitical prohibition.[9]
And despite the frequent mention of male cult prostitutes in
deuteronomic history, no prophet associates this practice
with the nation's fall. In fact, George Edwards observes, no
prophet mentions male cult prostitutes or discusses their
activity at all.[10]

A Deeper Exploration into the Meaning of Lev. 18:22

Still, the association of the Levitical prohibition of homosexual acts with idolatry is widely accepted by exegetes.[11]
On the other hand, Stephen Bigger understands cultic laws
not to be restricted to issues of idolatry. He sees the laws in
Lev. 18 as intending to discourage impurity on an individual
or communal level. Punishments such as those in Lev. 20
served to reinforce pollution belief. Pollution was seen as
contagious and brought people into real danger, which could
result in misfortune, sickness or death.

> *Pollution restrictions were not directly con-*
> *cerned with moral questions and most have*
> *no bearing on morality, but in some cases*
> *(such as sexual matters) morality was in*
> *practice encouraged by fear of pollution.*[12]

Fear of pollution may have prevented behavior that was
difficult to control because it was essentially private.

Bigger marks the Holiness Code as contemporary with

Ezekiel and formulated in Jerusalem. The Code found the reason for the contemporary misfortunes in the competing cults at a time when the power of Yahweh seemed questionable.[13]

The reference to idolatry in vs. 21 has caused commentators to confuse cultic issues and issues of idolatry when commenting on vs. 22. Rigger advances the discussion by showing how these two issues differ. Karl Elliger seeks to remove the issue of idolatry from discussion of the laws of Lev. 18 by showing that the verse mentioning idolatry is a later insertion. He sees Lev. 18 containing two groups of laws, the second group being found in a unit composed of vss. 17b-23. The verses in this unit mesh together in various ways, especially through their bringing family and sexual relations under the purview of the national cult. But vs. 21 is an exception, and was inserted later.[14] It was probably inserted by the final editor of the chapter, who added the framework, vss. 1-5 and 24-30. This verse and these two sections are united by the phrase, "I am Yahweh." Elliger suggests that this editor was a contemporary of Ezekiel.[15] The grouping of the two sets of laws, vss. 6-17a and 17b-23, predates Ezekiel and the second set did not originally include the reference to idolatry now in vs. 21.

The first group of laws forbid sexual contact within certain limits of kinship. The second group relates various other forbidden sexual contacts. The two units are brought together by the similar phrasing of vss. 6 and 17b.[16] Elliger places the laws in ch. 18 in an earlier setting, at a time when extended families could no longer protect themselves, but derived protection from the community through its cultic ability. By observing purity the community would secure its divine favor and its character of holiness.[17]

Further evidence that the laws of Lev.18 do not have to do with idolatry comes from R. J. Porter. Porter points out that the theology of the Holiness Code in general holds that the nation's holiness depended not so much on the purity of

the temple and cult as with the social and ethical duties of
the ordinary Israelite. Most of the laws are apodictic; violation of them is unthinkable. The death penalty is frequently
prescribed, as in the case of homosexuality between males
(cf. Lev. 20:13). This prescription probably reflects the
seriousness of law-breaking more than actual penal practice.[18]   Porter places the origin of many of the individual
units of the Code at various Israelite shrines. Much of the
material is from a very early date, well before the exile, before Jerusalem emerged as the sole national sanctuary.

X ____The homosexual offense relates to infringement of proper
order, according to Porter, who refers the reader to the dietary laws.[19] Ritual purity in dietary laws and elsewhere involves completeness or perfection. If something in one category takes on the characteristics of another category,
imperfection and confusion ensues, and the proper order of
the world is destroyed. This guarding of categories is the
basis for the distinction of clean and unclean animals. This
thinking is reflected in the priestly theology of Gen. 1, where
the different orders and kinds of the world are created by
acts of separation.[20]

Bestiality (Lev. 18:23) is condemned as a confusion
(*tebel*), since, as Wenham points out, it is a transgression of
God-given boundaries. "Holiness in the Pentateuch is a
matter of purity, of keeping apart what God has created to
be separate."[21]   He cites other laws forbidding mixtures
which are considered unnatural: Lev. 19:19 rf. cross-breeding
of cattle,[22] sowing a field with two kinds of seed, wearing
cloth made with blended fabrics; Deut. 22:5 rf. male or
female transvestism: Deut. 22:9-11 rf. sowing vineyard with
two kinds of seed, hitching an ox with an ass, wearing wool
and linen together.[23]

The same point regarding mixing of categories is made in
a brief article by C. Houtman. He gives prominence to the
creation story, in which each different order is set up
"according to its kind." Since the habitable universe has

come into being via acts of separation, blurring the separation may induce the reversion to chaos, and which must be prevented.[24]   Yet while Houtman sees the theology of the Priestly creation story (order through distinct categories) as the foundation of these laws, he fails to point out that Dueteronomy and the Holiness Code, and particularly older units within the Code, must be seen as prior to P. Genesis 1 systematically illustrates the theology which found earlier expression in these laws.

The laws concerning the separation of kinds and the dietary laws form part of the context for understanding Lev. 18: 22. Laws in the immediate context include vs. 19, forbidding sexual contact with a menstruating woman; vs. 20, warning against defilement by sexual contact with one's neighbor's wife; and vs. 23, against bestiality. These, together with lying "with a male as with a woman," are forbidden forms of sexual contact.   The contention that the issue of misuse of semen is involved in vs. 22 should be removed from consideration, since the Old Testament law contains no injunction against masturbation, and Lev. 15:16-17 indicates that contact with semen was a relatively minor matter.[25]   However, the question of sexual contact with a menstruating woman in association with the issue of homosexuality should alert our criticial judgment.   Today we can see contact with a menstruating woman clearly as a ritual cleanliness issue, irrelevant to Christian morality. But John Noonan points out that up until the late eighteenth century, Catholic moral theologians considered such contact a mortal sin.[26]

Elliger's suggestion that vs. 21 does not form part of the original unit, removing the association with idolatry from the immediate literary context of vs. 22, further clarifies the meaning of "abomination" in vs. 22. When the issue of purity is brought to the fore, the term abomination loses its association with idolatry, since defilement rather than idolatry is clearly the theme surrounding the four uses of "abomination" in 18:26-30.

Mary Douglas suggests another reason why the prohibition of practices as foreign ought not to be too quickly explained by their association with foreign cults. Explaining by the use of this association does not tell why some pagan practices were allowed, and some were even made central in the cult of Yahweh.

> Any interpretations will fail which take the do-
> nots of the Old Testament in piecemeal fashion
> .... Since each of the injunctions is prefaced by
> the command to be holy, so they must be ex-
> plained by that command. There must be
> contrariness between holiness and abomination
> which will make overall sense of all the par-
> ticular restrictions.[27]

Her approach to Leviticus is canonical; she treats the received text as the sacred text of a community rather than searching out the background of specific sections. But her analysis of holiness and purity are consistent with what we have seen to be the concerns of the Holiness Code. Her point is basically the same as we have already seen in Porter and Houtman, but she explores the basis and consequences of it more thoroughly.

Ideas about separating, purifying, demarcating and punishing transgressions impose order on an inherently untidy experience, Douglas points out.[28] The guidelines for imposing order are derived from a view of the universe where some things are subject to restrictions and others are not. The Latin word *sacer* has the meaning of restriction, though pertaining to the gods. Similarly, the Hebrew root *k-d-sh*, usually translated as "holy," is based on the idea of separation. "I am set apart and you must be set apart like me" (Lev. 11:46 Ronald Knox translation).[29]

Ideas about dirt, notes Douglas, are part of symbolic systems. Dirt is simply matter out of place. The existence of dirt implies two conditions: a set of ordered relationships, and a contravention of that order. Dirt is never an isolated event. Where there is dirt, there is a system. Dirt is the by-product of systematizing, insofar as ordering involves rejecting inappropriate elements. Pollution behavior is the reaction which condemns any object or idea likely to confuse or contradict cherished classifications.[30]

The idea of order reflected in the levitical view of holiness is associated with wholeness and completeness. In Lev. 21:17-21 the priest must be a [physically] perfect man. Holiness was given an external, physical expression in the wholeness of the body as a perfect container. As a result, any contact with bodily discharges defiles.[31] Holiness requires that individuals conform to the class to which they belong, and that the different classes of things not be confused. Therefore, holiness demanded that confusions such as breeding hybrid plants and animals be forbidden. Regarding incest, holiness is more a matter of separating that which should be separated than protecting the rights of husbands and brothers.[32] The most compelling validation of Douglas' theory lies in the way she explains the dietary laws of Lev. 11. She discerns a pure class for each type of clean animal and shows how the unclean animals are grouped according to the way they fail to conform to this class.[33]

The four laws in Lev. 18:19-23 (following Elliger in excluding vs. 21) clearly follow Douglas' theory of cleanliness. The prohibition against intercourse with a menstruating woman in vs. 19 regards the body as a perfect vessel, a view in which all bodily discharges cause defilement. The prohibition of adultery in vs. 20 is not mentioned as sin, but as defilement, since it confuses the category of wife. Vs. 22 tells us what sort of defilement homosexual acts are: "You shall not lie with a *male* as with a *woman*." The italicized words here are taken from two different systems of categorization. We have neither the biological pair of male and female (Gen. 1:27) nor the human pair of man and woman

(Gen. 2:23). Since the former pair of words usually applies to animals (Gen. 7:3), and the context here does not call for a word referring to an animal (quite the contrary, since the next verse talks about bestiality, clarity would be served by the use of a term indicating a *human* male), the language suggests that the violation of order lies with the "male." Here a male is not conforming to his class, but acting as a woman.[34] The law may be read specifically to forbid anal intercourse between men, and may be understood in relationship to the law forbidding transvestism either in men or women (Deut. 22:5) also an abomination. We may speculate that sexual acts between women are not mentioned because in such acts neither woman acts as a man. We have already seen the treatment of bestiality as a confusion, vs. 23. That this is a cleanliness issue rather than a straightforward moral issue is seen in the fact that the beast involved is to be killed as well (Lev. 20:15-16).

Applying Lev. 18:22 to Ethical Discussion

Douglas tries to understand why ideas of sacred contagion flourished in the same societies and not in others. Her distinction helps us to address the hermeneutical problems in applying Lev. 18:22 to the contemporary situation. The criterion for whether ideas of sacred contagion dominate a society is based on the Kantian principle that thought can only advance by freeing itself from the shackles of its own subjective conditions. The Copernican revolution is renewed continually as we realize new ways in which our subjective viewpoint makes us the center of the universe. Our culture needs to be distinguished from others which lack this type of objectivity.[35]

In a culture which lacks this critical view, individuals see the universe as part of themselves in a complementary way. The universe is human-centered and can be interpreted with reference to human beings. So with astrology, the subject is linked to cosmic forces. The universe is personal and is expected to behave as if it were responsive to our signs, symbols ang gestures, as if it could discern social relationships. The universe may be expect to discern, for example, whether partners in sexual intercourse are related within the prohibited degrees. In other words, the universe discerns the social order and intervenes to uphold it.[36] The polluting person is then a danger to society, and the threat of danger serves as a deterrent where enforcement is otherwise difficult. The polluting person is always in the wrong, regardless of intention.[37] Thus, in this atmosphere, where the individual is intimately linked to cosmic forces, ideas of sacred contagion flourish, while such ideas become irrevelant as the subject becomes differentiated from the cosmos.

This explanation clarifies why, in the repression against homosexual acts which occurred in the late Roman Empire under Christian auspices, Christian authorities invoked not Paul or Leviticus, but the Sodom story.[38] The fate of Sodom illustrated the perceived danger posed when anyone violated this purity regulation. This explanation also tells why the so-called pro-family groups today set themselves in opposition to gay rights. There would be no need for pro-family groups if individuals did not perceive their understanding of the category of "family" to be transgressed. They seek to protect the category of "family" by repressing those who do not fit into their definition of the category. They project responsibility for the problems of the family on gay and lesbian people.[39] While the oppression of lesbian and gay people does not reduce their numbers, and in fact alienates gays and lesbians from their own families, the violence done to families of lesbians and gays is justified in the view of the pro-family groups. The traditional definition of the family is protected. If the families of gay and lesbian people are torn apart as a result, the "pro-family" forces may reason, "The operation was a success, but the patient died."

While prohibitions against hybreding cattle, transvestism, or intercourse with a menstruating woman are no longer seen as morally relevant, prohibitions against incest, adultery and bestiality still have moral value today. The fact that these laws are found within various Old Testament codes is not sufficient cause for considering them binding on Christians. For example, while the ethical laws from the Jewish scriptures were largely accepted into Christianity, cleanliness laws such as ritual washings (Mk. 7:1-23, par.) or dietary laws (Acts 10: 9-16) were not.

In the case of laws regarding sexual matters, it is often more difficult to distinguish ritual from ethical regulations. One of the reviewers of Boswell's book has noted that sexual prohibitions tend to have a longer life than other ritual prohibitions. They are notoriously capable of surviving the dissolution of taboo structures like the Holiness Code and reappearing in later moral codes.[40] The prohibition against intercourse with a menstruating woman, which occurs three verses before the prohibition of homosexual acts between males, is a case in point. Only relatively recently have Christian ethicists come to see the former as a ritual cleanliness restriction which need not be considered binding.

I have shown that the reasoning which underlies the prohibition of homosexual acts between males in Lev. 18:22 is also ritual cleanliness reasoning. Since Christianity does not in general bind itself to Levitical cleanliness laws, and since their prescientific rationale is incompatible with modern, post-Kantian ways of thought, it is arbitrary to continue to accept some cleanliness laws as authoritative. Because Christian morality is not based on ritual cleanliness, Christian ethical arguments should not have recourse to ritual cleanliness laws.

This is not to advocate an antinomian attitude toward matters mentioned in codes like the Holiness Code. Acts such as adultery (Lev. 18:20) or bestiality (Lev. 18:23) are unacceptable to Christians for reasons other than that they cause ritual defilement. Likewise, any argument which might be made concerning the moral acceptability or unacceptability of homosexual acts must be grounded in reasons other than concern for ritual cleanliness. Even to use Lev. 18:22 to illustrate a moral argument that has been grounded elsewhere gives this law more authority than it should have in a modern Chrisian context.

—Thomas M. Thurston, Ph.D.

NOTES

[1] Derrick Sherwin Bailey, *Homosexuality and the Western Christian Tradition* (New York: Longmans, Green and Co., 1955), pp. 29-37.

[2] *Ibid.*

[3] John Boswell, *Christianity, Social Tolerance and Homosexuality* (Chicago: University of Chicago Press, 1980), pp. 100-101. Boswell points out (p. 101, n. 32) that the Mishnah and the Jewish community did not regard the stated punishment or lack thereof associated with a particular law as an index of its moral gravity.

[4] *Ibid.*, pp. 102-3.

[5] *Ibid.*, pp. 104-5. In Bailey's findings, it was not the Levitical condemnation, nor even Paul, which was used in the early Church in the biblical argument against homosexuality, but the Sodom story. Bailey, pp. 82-83. David Wright, "Homosexuals or Prostitutes? The Meaning of ARSENO-KOITAI [I Cor. 6:9, I Tim. 1:10]," in *Vigiliae Christianae* 38 (1984), pp. 130-131, contends that the Pauline term $\alpha\rho\sigma\epsilon\nu o\kappa o\iota\tau\alpha\iota$ is based on the LXX rendering of Lev. 18.22, and he is critical of Boswell for overlooking this connection, since Boswell is clearly familiar with the LXX here. Wright's

arguments on the etymology of αροενκοιται are convincing.

[6] Tom Horner, *Jonathan Loved David: Homosexuality in Biblical Times* (Philadelphia: The Westminster Press, 1978), pp. 77-8.

[7] *Ibid.*, p. 65.

[8] *Ibid.*, p. 66. cf. Bailey, p. 53.

[9] Robin Scroggs, *The New Testament and Homosexuality* (Philadelphia: Fortress Press, 1983), p. 73.

[10] George R. Edwards, *Gay/Lesbian Liberation: a Biblical Perspective* (New York: Pilgrim Press, 1984), p. 64. Hosea 4: 4 attacks female cult prostitutes, Edwards, p. 61.

[11] *E.g.*: Stephen F. Bigger, "The Family Laws of Leviticus 18 in their Setting," in *Journal of Biblical Literature* 98 (1979), 202-3; N. H. Snaith, *Leviticus and Numbers / The Century Bible* (London: Thomas Nelson and Sons, Ltd., 1967), p. 126; Walter Kornfeld, *Levitikus, Die Neue Echter Bibel* (Stuttgart. Echter Verlag, 1980), p. 71.

[12] Bigger, p. 195.

[13] *Ibid.*, p. 203.

[14] Karl Elliger, "Das Gesetz Leviticus 18," in *Zeitschrift für die alttestamentliche Wissenschaft* 67 (1955), p. 17.

[15] *Ibid.*, p. 24.

[16] *Ibid.*, p. 16.

[17] *Ibid.*, p. 17.

[18] J. R. Porter, *Leviticus* (Cambridge: Cambridge University Press, 1976), pp. 134-5. Bamberger notes that there is no record of a death sentence for this offense ever being carried out under Jewish auspices. Bernard J. Bamberger, *Leviticus, The Torah: A Modern Commentary* vol. 3 (New York: Union of American Hebrew Congregations, 1977), p. 189.

[19] Porter, 148.

[20] *Ibid.*, p. 84.

[21] Gordon J. Wenham, *The Book of Leviticus* (Grand Rapids, MI: William H. Eerdmans Publishing Co., 1979), pp. 259-60.

[22] John Boswell notes that Maimonides specifically and repeatedly equated homosexual acts with matters like the hybridization of cattle, cf. Boswell, p. 101, n. 32.

[23] Wenham, p. 260.

[24] C. Houtman, "Another Look at Forbidden Mixtures," in *Vetus Testamentum* 34.2 (1984), pp. 227-8.

[25] Porter suggests that this passage is more recent than Lev. 18:17-23, since in Lev. 15:24, the punishment for intercourse with a menstruating woman is considerably toned down, from the death penalty in 20:18 to seven days of uncleanness.

[26] John T. Noonan, Jr., *Contraception: A History of Its Treatment by the Catholic Theologians and Canonists* (Cambridge, MA: Harvard University Press, 1965), p. 440, n. 6.

[27] Mary Douglas, *Purity and Danger: An Analysis of the Concept of Purity and Taboo* (New York: Praeger, 1966), p. 49.

[28] *Ibid.*, p. 4.

[29] *Ibid.*, p. 8.

[30] *Ibid.*, pp. 35-6.

[31] *Ibid.*, p. 51.

[32] *Ibid.*, p. 53.

[33] *Ibid.*, pp. 55-7.

[34] In this sense, John McNeill's interpretation of this passage is basically correct. However, while he finds the prohibition linked to misogyny, I do not find this connection necessary.

[35] *Ibid.*, p. 78.

[36] *Ibid.*, pp. 82-7.

[37] *Ibid.*, p. 113.

[38] Bailey, *op. cit.*, p. 80.

[39] The recent Vatican document "On the Pastoral Care of Homosexual Persons" (PCHP, Congregation for the Doctrine of the Faith [October 1, 1986]; "Homosexualitatis problema," *Acta Apostolicae Sedis, Commentarium officiale* 79:5 [May 5, 1987), pp. 543-4.) paragraph 9 envisions the threat that gay and lesbian people pose to family life on the level of ideas. John R. Quinn, "Toward and Understanding of the Letter 'On the Pastoral Care of Homosexual Persons,' *America* 155:15 (November 22, 1986), p. 314, claims that PCHP was written because of the threat that certain gay militants pose to family life.

[40]Jeremy DuQ. Adams in *Speculum* 56 (1981) p. 351, as cited in David F. Wright, "Homosexuals or Prostitutes? The Meaning of ARSENOKOITAI (I Cor. 6:9; I Tim. 1.10)," in *Vigiliae Christianae* 38 (1984), p. 129.

Early Jewish and Christian Attitudes toward
Male Homosexuality as Expressed in the
Testament of Naphtali

The foundational documents of Post-Biblical Judaism and Christianity do not offer us pictures of gay men as a distinct group within ancient society. The contemporary understanding of sexual minorities, groups defined by their sexual orientation, is not reflected in Jewish canonical and non-canonical literature, in the NT and early Christian writings and in the rabbinic corpus. There is no discussion of gay men in this broad literature as there is, for example, of slaves, of women, of gentiles, and of members of various social classes and occupations. In other words, there are no gay men for the early Church and the early Synagogue; there are only men who engage in sexual relations with other men.

Concepts such as (1) an individual's sexual orientation and (2) sexuality as being inherent in a person are foreign to these texts. Rather, they describe the sources of human sexual desire as external to the person. People react to external stimuli. For example, women, in this understanding, present a danger to men who are trying to live righteous lives. It is not because women are inherently evil but because their mere presence causes desire, *porneia*, an external agent, to grab hold of the man (*T. Reub.* 3:10; 4:1; 5:6; *T. Jud.* 17:1; *T. Iss.* 4:4; *T. Benj.* 8:2-3).[1] Therefore, all sexual activity is potentially dangerous for it opens up the individual to foreign possession. However, certain forms of sexual activity —sexual relations for the purpose of procreation (*T. Iss.* 2)— within certain social structures—marriage (*T. Reub.* 4:1)— were permitted and often fostered. The institution of marriage and the requirement to procreate were understood as part of the natural order of creation (Gen. 1-2).

The usefulness of ancient materials for developing a new understanding of gay life, particularly its most intimate aspects, within a Western Religious context is limited. There is no text or subtext from this early period that would permit us to recreate a vision of early Christianity or early Judaism from the gay perspective. One can neither write a counter-history about a movement submerged by modern prejudices and academic conventions in the order of Gershom Scholem's studies in Jewish mysticism nor recreate the experiences of a central but suppressed group as modern feminist scholars have done for women from all periods.

Similarly, the apparently straight forward prohibitions against male-male sexual relations limit our ability to base a pattern of sexual activity on these sources that would answer the needs of those outside of the heterosexual community. The task of the contemporary reader, sympathetic to the needs of gay men and women, is not to approach the material apologetically. Rather, it is to present the material, to the best of his or her ability, within its own context and in light of its own suppositions.

The assumption that early Jewish and Christian literature took an absolutist position against sexual relations between men has been challenged in two recent studies: John Boswell's *Christianity, Social Tolerance and Homosexuality,* and Robin Scorggs's *The New Testament and Homosexuality.*[2] Both authors conclude that the New Testament and related writings do not address homosexuality in its modern form. Scroggs sees the discussion regarding homosexuality in the New Testament to refer to a form of exploitative pederasty.[3] Boswell holds that the New Testament—particularly, Paul's epistles—does not condemn homosexuals but rather "homosexual acts committed by heterosexual persons."[4]

An analysis of the third and fourth chapters of the Testament of Naphtali (*T. Naph.*), one of the Testaments of the Twelve Patriarchs (*T. 12 Patr.*), indicates that one cannot maintain Scroggs' or Boswell's positions with respect to the early Jewish and Christian parenesis typified by the Testaments. *T. Naph.* articulates a clear position against sexual relations between men that fits the attitudes against sexuality expressed in the *T. 12 Patr.* in particular and in early Judaism and Christianity in general.

The *T. 12 Patr.* is particularly revealing witness to the manner in which early Jews and early Christians interpreted their scriptural heritage. It reflects the way in which the early Church was able to incorporate Jewish material with only minor readjustments. The Testaments appear to be addressed to an audience of believers. They do not seek to explain the faith to outsiders but rather to instruct those within. The literary device of the final testaments of the twelve sons of Jacob serve to bind the *T. 12 Patr.* to Israel's scriptural heritage. Although the *T. 12 Patr.* is outside the canon for both Jews and Christians, it reflects the fashion in which early Jews and Christians read and taught canonical scripture.[5]

The argument that authors of the *T. 12 Patr.* objected to sexual relations between men is based: (1) on references to Sodom in the Testaments and contemporaneous literature, (2) on the use of the Greek terms *taxis* and *physis* in that literature, and (3) on the fact that male-male sexual relations were considered to be a form of illicit sexual desire: *porneia.*

Although the authors of the *T. 12 Patr.* were opposed to sexual relations between men, they do not seem to have considered such relations to be a major problem. In contrast to their strong condemnation of irregular heterosexual relationships in the *T. 12 Patr.*, their relative lack of interest in homosexual relations seems out of place.

The issue of sexual relations between men is not stressed in the *T. 12 Patr.* The crucial words which form the basis of the current research into attitudes concerning sexual relationships between members of the same sex, particularly between men, do not appear in the testaments. These words include: *kalos* (beautiful), *pais* (youth), *eromenos* (beloved), *erastes* (lover), *eros* (love), *malakos* (effeminate, soft), *arsenokoites* (one who has intercourse with a man), and *paiderastia* (the love of youths).[6]

The relative lack of interest in sexual relations between members of the same sex in the *T. 12 Patr.* testifies that such behavior was not seen as a major problem. The few contemporaneous Jewish sources which deal with the issue condemn such relationships but see them for the most part as a gentile, not a Jewish vice.[7]

A similar lack of interest in the issue of sexual relations between men appears as well in the New Testament. Robin Scroggs, holding an extreme position, claims that "in comparison with the abundance of materials about pederasty in Greco-Roman literature, the New Testament is virtually silent .... For the churches which produced the Gospels, homosexuality was obviously not an issue at all; there is not a single statement about it in any of these writings. The Book of Acts certainly and the Revelation of John most probably do not mention it. Only in the epistolary literature does the issue explicitly emerge, and at that, only three times. (1 Cor. 6:9019; Rom. 1:26-27; 1 Tim. 1:9-10)."[8]

The general rejection of sexuality in the *T. 12 Patr.* appears to apply to homosexuality as well as to heterosexuality. Commenting on a similar phenomenon in a much broader range of literature, John Boswell concludes his survey of attitudes towards homosexuality in the NT and patristic tradition with the warning: "One must be careful, moreover, not to confuse hostility to same-sex eroticism in particular with hostility to eroticism in general."[9]

This observation is of particular importance for contemporary moralists attempting to use their religious tradition to develop a modern approach to sexual issues, particularly homosexuality. Boswell asks his readers: "...to remember that where such authorities explicitly condemned homosexuality, they also categorically rejected the majority of human sexual experience."[10] The theological and moral issue is, then, not homosexuality specifically, but rather the appoach to sexuality in general.

The historian's task is to demonstrate and then explan the attitudes to all forms of sexuality including homosexuality. The *T. 12 Patr.* does not provide a great deal of information concerning homosexuality beyond testifying to the belief that sexual relations between men are forbidden and associated conceptually with idolatry.[11] The evidence of the *T. 12 Patr.* calls into question Scroggs' opinion that the real concern in the NT and the contemporaneous Jewish literature is with exploitative pederasty and Boswell's contention that "the New Testament takes no demonstrable position on homosexuality."[12]

T. Naph. 3:1-4:2

Do not, then, be goaded into wrong-doing by covetousness, neither deceive yourselves with empty words, because if you keep silent in purity of heart you will understand how to hold fast God's will and reject the devil's. 2. Sun, moon and stars do not change their order: so too you must not change the law of God by disorderliness of what you do. 3. The Gentiles went astray and forsook the Lord and changed their order, and they went after stones and stocks, led away by spirits of error. 4. But you will not be so, my children: you have recognized in the vault of heaven, and in the earth, and in the sea, and in all created things, the Lord who made them all, so that you should not become like Sodom which changed the order of its nature. 5. Similarly; the Watchers also changed the order of their nature, and the Lord cursed them also at the flood, and it

> was *because of them* that *he made the earth
> a waste, without inhabitants or fruit.*
>   *4:1. I am telling you this, my children
> because I have read in the holy writings of
> Enoch that you yourselves also will forsake
> the Lord and do the same wicked things that
> the Gentiles will do and behave like the law-
> less men of Sodom. 2. And the Lord will
> bring captivity upon you, and you will be
> slaves there to your enemies and subjected
> to every* kind of *hardship and ill-treatment
> until the Lord has made an end of you alto-
> gether.*[13]

What is the sin or the sins that will cast Naphtali's descendants into exile? Read literally, 4:1 says: "following all
the wickedness of the Gentiles (*poreuomenoi kata ponerian
ethnon*), you [Naphtali's descendants] will do all the lawlessness of Sodom (*kai poiesete kata pasan anomian Sodomon*)."
T. Naph 3:3 identifies "all the wickedness of the Gentiles" as
idolatry.[14] The heart of the problem is identifying the "lawlessness of Sodom."

The common understanding is that Sodom was destroyed
because of the depravity of its inhabitants. For us, the issue
is clouded by the use of the English word "sodomy" which
derives ultimately from *Sodoma*, the Latin form of the Hebrew word *Sodom*, and reflects the traditional reading of the
Sodomites' sin in sexual terms. The term, "sodomy," bears a
range of meanings which runs from anal copulation of one
man with another to anal or oral copulation in general to
sexual acts with animals.[15]

As the archtypical sinful city in the biblical and post-
biblical traditions, Sodom and its inhabitants could be and
were accused of any or all sins. It is not the case that the
Sodomites were guilty of one sin to the exclusion of all
others.   Rather, the specific sin or sins stressed in any one

source reflects that source's specific concerns.

Gen. 19 illustrates the utter wickedness of the Sodomites by describing the attempt of the men of Sodom to rape, *en masse*, the two angelic figures who arrived in the form of men to warn Abraham's nephew, Lot, of the forthcoming destruction of the city. In this light, the attempt to rape the visitors is not the specific sin of the Sodomites but is emblematic of their general sinfulness.

Elsewhere in the Hebrew Bible the condemnation of the Sodomites does not focus on their sexual transgressions. For example, in the prophetic writings the Sodomites stand condemned of a variety of crimes, including: lacking justice (Isa. 1:10; 3:9), disregarding moral and ethical values (Jer. 23:14), and ignoring the impoverished (Ezek. 16:48-49).[16]

Similarly, Rabbinic interpretation of the Sodomites wickedness does not focus solely on their sexual irregularities. The Sodomites are often described as mean, inhospitable, uncharitable and unjust (*b. Sanh.* 109a; *b. Ketub.* 103a; *b. B.Bat.* 12b, 59a, 168a; *b. Erub.* 49a). Some midrashic sources, however, characterize the evil that was found in Sodom as sexual transgressions (*Lev. Rab.* 23.9; *Gen. Rab.* 26.5, 50.5).[17]

In particular, the Targums, early Jewish translations of the Bible into Aramaic, present the sin of Sodom as sexual sin. For example, one Targum from Palestine, *Targum Pseudo-Jonathan*, translates the Hebrew verb *y-d-c* "to know" with the Aramaic verb *š-m-š*: "to serve," or "to have sexual relations." However, not all the targums are so explicit. *Targum Neofiti*, another Palestinian Jewish Aramaic translation, more closely reflects the Hebrew original by using the more ambiguous Aramaic term *h-k-m*, "to be wise," which bears the same metaphoric meaning of "to have sexual intercourse" as does the Hebrew *y-d-c*.[18]

As in the Bible and in rabbinic literature, the Apocrypha and Pseudepigrapha there is no one understanding of what were the sins of Sodom.[19] *Ben Sira* holds that the sin of pride was the cause of the overthow of Sodom (Sir. 16:8).

The *Wisdom of Solomon* attributes it to the inhabitants' inhospitality (*Wis.* 19:15-17). In *Jubilees* the Sodomites were guilty of unspecified sexual sins and pollutions (*Jub.* 16.5-6 and 20:5-6). The warning against allowing women to be sexually loose and against intermarriage with Canaanite women in *Jub.* 20.4 suggests that the sexual behaviors warned against (*Jub.* 20:5) are heterosexual in nature.

The clearest descriptions of the sin of Sodom as sexual acts between men appear in *2 Enoch*. In 10:4 the behavior of Sodom is described as "a sin which is against nature, which is child corruption in the anus in the manner of Sodom;" and in 34:2, as "friend with friend in the anus." Though *2 Enoch* stems from the first century C.E., it is an unreliable witness. It survives only in a number of later Slavonic versions with no extant manuscript older than the fourteenth century and the explicit descriptions of the Sodomite's sin come from one manuscript of the longest version.[20]

Other contemporaneous sources associate the sins of the generation of the Watchers and their gigantic children with the sins of Sodom and Gomorrah. *Jub* 20:5-6 compares the Sodomites and the giants. In *Sir* 16:7-10, the sage uses the examples of the giants, the Sodomites and the generation of the desert-wandering as examples of God's willingness to punish sinners. *3 Macc.* 2:4-6 holds that insolence and pride were the sin of not only the giants and the Sodomites but also of Pharaoh. *2 Pet.* 2:4-9 uses the example of the sinful angels, Noah's generation and the wickedness of Sodom and Gomorrah to argue that God has the power to rescue the righteous and punish the wicked.

Josephus and Philo describe the sins of the Sodomites explicitly as homosexual relations. Josephus claims that the men of Sodom were overcome by desire for Lot's angelic visitors because of their youthful beauty and wished to have sexual relations with them (*Ant.* I:199-204). Philo uses the story of Sodom to present a strong polemic against homosexuality in general (*de Abr.* 133-41; *Quaest. in Gen.* 4:3).[21]

The other references to Sodom in *T. 12 Patr.*, the *Testament of Benjamin* (*T. Benj.*) 9:1, the *Testament of Levi* (*T. Levi*) 14:6, and the *Testament of Asher* (*T. Ash.*) 7:1 point to an understanding of her sin as sexual relations between men. The clearest description of Sodom's wickedness in the *T. 12 Patr.*, besides *T. Naph.* 3:1-4:2, appears in *T. Benj.* 9:1:

> But I gather from the words of the righteous Enoch that you will give yourselves up to evil practices. For as the men of Sodom committed fornication (porneia), so also will you, and all but a few of you will perish. And you will renew your wanton relations with women; and the Lord's kingdom will not remain among you, for he himself will take it away from you immediately.

This passage clearly refers to a number of events in the history of the tribe of Benjamin concluding with the unfortunate reign of Saul. The patriarch describes the affair of the Levite and his concubine in the Benjaminite town of Gibeah (*Jdgs* 19) by comparing it to the treatment of the visitors in Sodom. As the men of Sodom wished to have sexual relations with Lot's visitors, so the men of Gibeah wished to have sexual relations with the visiting Levite. In both cases the men are offered women as substitutes.

Since the men of Gibeah rape and kill the Levite's concubine while the daughters of Lot are not harmed by the men of Sodom, the *porneia* both groups of men committed cannot be seen as heterosexual rape. Rather, it must refer to the desire of both the Sodomites and Benjaminites to engage in sexual relations with their male guests.

The prediction that the Benjaminites will renew their "wanton relations with women" does not argue against this interpretation. Rather, it refers to the replenishing of the tribe of Bejamin by their marriage to the women survivors of the raid of Jabesh and the rape of the women of Shilo (*Jdgs* 21).

In *T. Levi* 14:6, the patriarch, Levi, predicts that his descendants will commit a number of different sexual sins. He warns his sons, saying: "You will pollute married women and defile the daughters of Jerusalem, and you will be united with prostitutes and adulteresses. You will take Gentile women as wives and purify them with a *form of* purification contrary to the law; and your unions will be like Sodom and Gomorrah in ungodliness."

Although it is easy to identify most of the sexual sins mentioned in this passage as adultery, intermarriage, and other forms of extramarital and illegitimate sex, it is not as readily apparent as to what Levi means by comparing the "unions'" of his sons with those of the men of Sodom and Gomorrah.[22] However, other contemporaneous Jewish sources indicate that the "union" can be best understood as male-male sexual relations.

This association of the sins of adultery and intermarriage with the sins of Sodom, however, is not restricted to *T. Levi.* For example, Philo's description of the sins of the Sodomites in *Abr* 133-41 typifies this association of adultery and homosexual relations. Philo claims, "Not only in their mad lust for women did they violate the marriages of their neighbours but men mounted males without respect for the sex nature which the active partner shares with the passive." In addition, Greek language Jewish moral exhortations often bring together their condemnation of adultery and sexual relationships between men (*Sybilline Oracle* (*Sib. Or.*) 4:34, 5:166, 386-97 and 430; *Pseudo-Phocylides* (*Ps. Phocyl.*) 3).[23] In this light, it appears that the patriarch includes homosexual intercourse in his list of sexual transgressions.

The final reference to Sodom in the *T. 12 Patr.*, outside of *T. Naph.* appears in *T. Ash.* 7:1. There the patriarch advises his sons not to be like Sodom "which did not recognize the Lord's angels." Since the theme of the *T. Ash* is the exposition of the "Doctrine of the Two Ways, of good and evil," Asher is not speaking of sexual sins in particular. Rather, he employs the particular case of the Sodomites' inability to see the visitors as the angels they truly were as an illustration in moral blindness in general.

Thus it appears that the expression "the lawlessness of Sodom" in *T. Naph.* 4:1, most likely refers to sexual relationships between men. The issue of concern in the previous chapter, *T. Naph.* 3, however, is not proper sexual behavior but rather consistency with God's will. The patriarch, Naphtali, begins his address to his sons with the admonition that they should hold fast to God's will and reject the will of Beliar (the devil). He instructs them to avoid the corrupting influence of avarice (*pleonexia*) (see also *T. Levi* 14:6) and empty words (*logous kenous*). Although Nephtali does not specifically warn them about the dangers of sexual desire (*porneia*), it appears in the *Testament of Simon* (*T. Sim.* 5: 3-6) as one of the powers that draws the individual away from God and brings him close to the devil.

The contrast in the third chapter of *T. Naph.* is between that which is stable and that which is not. Knowing what is stable should provide one with the knowledge of the Lord. The order of the heavenly bodies exemplify stability. As the celestial bodies are subject to God's will, so one should be obedient to God's law (*T. Naph.* 3:2). The critical words in this context are *taxis* and *ataxis* ("order" and "disorder").

In the previous chapter, *T. Naph.* 2, the patriarch already argued that the structure of the human body reflects God's sense of order (2:8). He warned his children that they are, therefore, to conform to this good order as part of respecting God (2:9). Here, he argues that knowledge of God's work in creation should lead one to obey God's will (3:4). Both the microcosm (the body), and the macrocosm (creation) reflect the divine order.

Naphtali gives three examples of beings who turned away from this knowledge: the Gentiles, the Sodomites, and the

Watchers. Of the three, the passage only identifies the sin of the Gentiles, which is idolatry. The Gentiles are accused of changing their order (*taxis*) by going after things of stone and wood, that is, obeying the spirits of error (cf. Deut. 4:19). Although the sins of the Sodomites and the Watchers are not explicitly described, both groups are accused of the same crime: "changing the order of one's *physis*, nature" (*enallassein taxin physeos autou*) (*T. Naph.* 3:4-5).

In the Biblical account, the divine beings (*bny lhym*) who are called "the Watchers" in post-Biblical literature, are condemned for leaving their heavenly abode and cavorting with women (Gen. 6:1-11, 8:1-4, 12:3; 15; 19:1-3; 86:1-6; 88:1-3; 100:4; 106-107; 1 *QapGen.* 2:1-7; *I Pet.* 3:3-5; *1 Tim.* 2:9).

Although the concept of *physis* in its philosophic sense was employed in antiquity in the discussion of homosexuality,[24] one need not resort to philosophic usage to understand this passage.[25] In the more popular literature produced by Jews and early Christians, the term *physis* is often used to refer specifically to sexual characteristics and sexual organs.[26] *Ps. Phocyl.* 187 admonishes that one should not cut off a "youth's masculine procreative faculty" (*paidosones physis arsen*).[27] In *Barnabas* the prohibition against eating the hyena is allegorically explained as a prohibition against adultery and *porneia*, because "the hyena changes its nature every year becoming at one time male and at another time female" (*par' eniauton allassei ten physin*) (*Barn.* 10:7).

Understanding *physis* in the sense of sexual characteristics, the almost parallel expression in *T. Naph*, "*enallassein taxin physeos autou*," can be rendered, "to change the order of one's sexual nature." In terms of the Watchers, this means that these angels who were by nature sexless took on a sexual identity (cf. Matt. 22:30; Mark 12:25; Luke 20:36).[28]

In *T. Naph.* 3:4, the Sodomites are also accused of *enallassein taxin physeos autou*. In context of the above discussions on the interpretation of the sins of the Sodomites in the Apocyrpha and Pseudepigrapha and the meaning of the word *physis*, this phrase is best understood as describing homosexual relations. The use of the word *enallasso* in this passage strengthens this interpretation. In *Wis.* 14:26, as part of the attack on idolatry, idolaters are accused, among other crimes, of "the interchange of sex roles (*geneseos enallage*), irregular marriages, adultery and debauchery."[29]

Although it appears that to the authors of *T. Naph.* the Sodomites were guilty of sexual relations between men, the condemnation of such behavior does not play a major role in the *T. 12 Patr.* Even within *T. Naph.* male-male sexual relations are but one example, along with idolatry and general sexual misbehavior, of the type of activity that turns the individual away from God and towards the devil, Beliar.

It appears that to the authors of the *T. 12 Patr.* homosexual relations did not attract much attention. The major discussion of the issue is relegated to a Testament whose major concern is not sins of a sexual nature.[30]

The overriding concern of the *T. 12 Patr.* is to admonish its audience to remain faithful to God and loyal to God's ways. The righteous man was one who remained wholehearted with God and did not let himself fall under the influence of foreign and deceiving powers. Sexual desire, *porneia*, was seen as one of the powerful forces that draw men away from God. Therefore, it is not at all surprising that the *T. 12 Patr.* present a disapproving attitude toward male-male sexual relations along with other forbidden sexual activities (cf. *T. Benj.* 9:1).

Yet, the most extensive discussion of male-male sexual relations in the *T. 12 Patr., T. Naph.* 3:1-4:2, does not employ the concept of *porneia*. Rather, it describes male-male sexual relations as breaking the natural order. However, its contrast of God's will with the will of the devil and its warning that one can be lead stray by covetousness and empty words are contextually associated with the warning against *porneia* elsewhere in the *T. 12 Patr.* (*T. Levi* 14:6; *T. Sim.* 5: 3-6).

The condemnation of male-male sexual relations is a blanket condemnation. No distinctions are made between the active and passive partner. There is no discussion concerning the age of the individuals involved nor their sexual predilections.[31]

Admonitions against male-male sexual relations play a small role in the *T. 12 Patr.* The discussion of sexual issues in the Testaments centers on avoiding the entrapments of sexual desire, *porneia*. The *T. 12 Patr.* stress charity before and after marriage and present adultery as the most important sexual sin (*T. Jos.; T. Iss.; T. Jud.; T. Reub.*).

Compared to the clarity and extent of the condemnation of irregular heterosexual relationships in the *T. 12 Patr.*, one can conclude that the authors did not consider homosexual relationships to be as threatening. Why this is the case remains a matter of speculation but it may reflect the social situation of the *T. 12 Patr.*

Firstly, the *T. 12 Patr.* seems to have been addressed to a middle-class urban male audience, either Jewish or Christian, living in the urban centers of the eastern Mediterranean in the first two centuries C.E.[32] In these communities, male-male sexual relations were not seen as potentially destructive to the fabric of society as were adultery and pre-marital heterosexual intercourse. Homosexual relations may have been seen as a matter of personal impiety which did not threaten the stability of families and their relationships with other families in small, vulnerable communities in the same way as did adultery and pre-marital sexual intercourse.

Secondly, the *T. 12 Patr.*'s relative lack of concern with sexual relations between men may help identify the social status of its audience. Although the general Greco-Roman culture appears accepting of homosexual relations, such relations appear to be more common in aristocratic circles. Middle class entertainment, such as New Comedy, mime shows, and romance, show a much greater interest in heterosexual relationships and desire.[33]

Thirdly, in its condemnation of male-male sexual relations, the *T. 12 Patr.* reflects popular Hellenistic philosophic thought. The program of sexual ethics of the early Christians and Jews reflected in the *T. 12 Patr.* is similar to that of stoic moralists, such as Musonius Rufus.[34]

Finally, the Testaments promote the common belief that idolaters and not its readers, whether they were Jews or Christians, were guilty of such behaviors. This surely reflects the continuing polemic against idolatry in post-Biblical Jewish and early Christian writing as much as it does pagan practice. In this case, the accusation that idolaters are suspect of homosexuality strengthens the social distance between the early Jewish and Christian communities and their pagan neighbors.[35]

The *T. 12 Patr.* testify to a popular understanding of the scriptural heritage of Biblical Israel and the Apostolic Writings of the early Church. In this early period, sexual relations between men were among forbidden sexual activities. The Testaments do not permit a subtle reading of the material that would allow for certain forms of gay love under certain conditions as have been suggested for NT materials.

In this light, I believe that it would be false to the spirit of the early Jewish and early Christian communities that first heard and promoted scriptural teachings to argue that Old Testament and New Testament materials allow for sexual relations between men under any circumstances. Better, an acceptance of the discontinuities due to social change and to different understanding of human psychology and sexuality will allow a more honest reading of ancient materials and improve our ability to confront and to read the foundational documents of Western culture's religious traditions with a new freedom.

—Rabbi Lewis John Eron, Ph.D.

NOTES

[1] The term *porneia* is the crucial term for the understanding of human sexuality in the *T. 12 Patr.* It is ultimately derived from the Green verb *porneuo*, and is an abstract noun based on the word *porne* ("prostitute"). The Septuagint, the ancient Greek translation of the Old Testament, uses the word *porneia* and related terms to render words derived from the Hebrew root *z-n-h*.

The meaning of the term *porneia* goes beyond that of the English word for illicit sexual acts: "fornication." In the *T. 12 Patr.* it may refer to sexual activity (*T. Reub.* 5:5, 6:1; *T. Jud.* 15:1) but can also refer to sexual desire (*T. Reub* 6:6; *T. Jud* 13:2-3). *Porneia* appears as an outside force; hence it is important to protect oneself from its advances (*T. Reub.* 4:8, 11 and 6:1). At times this understanding of *porneia* is described as the spirit of *porneia* (*T. Reub.* 3:3) and at other times simply as *porneia*. See: Bruce Malina, "Does *Porneia* Mean 'Fornication'?" in *Novum Testamentum* 14 (1972), pp. 10-17; see also, J. Jensen, "Does *Porneia* Mean Fornication? A Critique of Bruce Malina," in *Novum Testamentum* 20 (1978), pp. 161-84.

[2] John Boswell, *Christianity, Social Tolerance and Homosexuality* (Chicago: University of Chicago Press, 1980); Robin Scroggs, *The New Testament and Homosexuality: Contextual Background for Contemporary Debate* (Philadelphia: Fortress Press, 1983).

[3] Robin Scroggs, *ibid.*, p. 126.

[4] John Boswell, *ibid.*, p. 109.

[5] For an extensive study of the history of modern studies of the *T. 12 Patr.*, see H. D. Slingerland, *The Testaments of*

Twelve Patriarchs, A Critical History of Research (SBL Monograph Series, vol. 21; Missoula, MT: Scholars, 1977).

There is as yet no concensus concerning the origins of the *T. 12 Patr.* Opinion ranges from viewing the Testaments as a Greek translation with Christian interpolations of a Jewish document written originally in Hebrew or Aramaic in the 1st century BCE Palestine (R. H. Charles, *The Greek Versions of the* Testaments of the Twelve Patriarchs, *Edited from Nine Mss. together with the Variants of the Armenian and Slavonic Versions and Some Hebrew Fragments* (Oxford: Clarendon, 1908), to understanding the Testaments as a text composed in Greek by a Christian author who employed Jewish sources (Marinus de Jonge, *The* Testaments of the Twelve Patriarchs: *A Study of Their Text, Composition and Origin* (Assen: van Gorcum, 1953)). Other scholars, such as Jurgen Becker, *Untersuchungen zur Entsehehunggsgeschichte der Testaments der Zwölf Patriarchen* (Arbeiten zur Geschichte des antiken Judentums ur des Urchristentums, vol. 8; Leiden: Brill, 1970), and Howard C. Kee, "The Ethical Dimensions of the *Testaments of the XII* as a Clue to Provenance," in *New Testament Studies* 24 (1978), pp. 259-70, find the origins of the *T. 12 Patr.* in Hellenistic Jewish communities.

The lack of concensus concerning the origins of the *T. 12 Patr.* as well as the close connections of style, form and content between the *T. 12 Patr.* and the broad range of early Jewish and Christian literature support the contention that the Testaments represent the shared heritage of Jewish and Christian moral teaching.

[6]John Boswell, *ibid*, pp. 41-59, 91-117. K. J. Dover, *Greek Homosexuality* (Cambridge, MA: Harvard University Press, 1978; New York. Vintage, 1980), pp. 15-17, 42-53.

The terms *paidophthoros* ("child seducer") and *ktenophthoros* ("beast seducer") appear in *T. Levi* 17:11 among a list of sinners who will appear in priestly circles in the fifth week of the seventh jubilee.

[7] Robin Scorggs, *ibid.*, pp. 97-98; cf. *Sib. Or.* 3:184, 595-600; 5:387, 429-31. Such an attitude appears in rabbinic literature as well (*m. Qidd.* 4:13; *t. Qidd.* 5.10; *Sifra Lev.* 18:3; *Lev. Rab.* 23.9; *Esth. Rab.* 3:2).

[8] Robin Scroggs, *ibid.*, pp. 99-100; Scroggs excludes the two closely related passages of Jude 6-13 and 2 Pet 2:4-18 because of the difficulty interpreting these passages. "The misconduct seems to be sexual in character, but the language used is so elusive as to make any certain judgement impossible." p. 100, n. 3.

Scroggs refers to J. N. D. Kelly, *The Epistles of Peter and of Jude* (New York: Harper and Row, 1969), pp. 258f, who argues that the "strange flesh" (*sarkos heteras*) in Jude 7 refers to the Sodomites lust for something not human (that is: the angels). Similarly, the angels of Gen. 6 lusted after women.

[9] John Boswell, *ibid.*, p. 164.

[10] John Boswell, *ibid.*, p. 165. Boswell cites Augustine, Jerome and Origen as examples of prominent Christian theologians who "...explicitly rejected eroticism as a positive human experience, insisting that sexuality should be divorced from pleasure in moral life and linked only to the function of procreation." p. 164.

[11] Robin Scroggs, *ibid.*, pp. 93-94.

[12] John Boswell, *ibid.*, p. 117.

[13] All translations: Marinus de Jonge, "The *Testaments of the Twelve Patriarchs*," in *The Apocryphal Old Testament*, edited by H. F. D. Sparks (Clarendon: Oxford, 1984), pp. 505-600.

[14] In the *T. 12 Patr.* idolatry and sexual desire (*porneia*) are often associated. See: *T. Reub.* 4:6; *T. Sim.* 5:3.

[15] *The American Heritage Dictionary*, 1227; John Boswell claims that this broad range of meaning makes the term "sodomy" useless in the study of homosexuality (Boswell, *ibid*, p. 93, n. 2). The association of "sodomy" with homosexual behavior is a medieval development. Boswell credits Peter Cantor (d. 1197) with interpreting Rom. 1:26-27 for the first time to refer "exclusively to gay people," and innovating the use of the term "sodomy" to refer "solely to homosexuality" (again against theological precedence); Boswell, *ibid.*, pp. 277, 375-8. The association of Sodom with homosexuality appears in the rules of the Third Lateran Council of 1179, known as the "first ecumenical ["general"] council to rule on homosexual acts" (Boswell, *ibid.*, p. 277, n. 26). Cf. John J. McNeill, *The Church and the Homosexual* (3d ed.; Boston: Beacon, 1988), pp. 75, 79-83.

[16] E. A. Speiser, *Genesis* (Anchor Bible vol. 1; Garden City, NY: Doubleday, 1964), p. 142. Although the specific condemnation of Sodom in Ezekiel centers on lack of concern for the poor (see also: Amos 4:1-12), the city of Jerusalem (which is compared to Sodom) is accused of idolatry and sexual immorality. Sodom is often used as a general symbol of evil (cf. Deut. 32:32) and destruction (cf. Deut. 29:23; Isa. 13.19; Jer. 50:40; Lam. 4:6; Zeph. 2:9).

[17] Marvin H. Pope, "Homosexuality," in *The Interpreter's Dictionary of the Bible, Supplementary Volume*, edited by Keith Crim (Nashville, TN: Abingdon, 1976), p. 415. Louis M. Epstein, *Sex Laws and Customs in Judaism* (New York: Bloch, 1948), pp. 134-8 for discussion of Rabbinic attitudes.

[18] Robin Scroggs, *ibid.*, pp. 73, 81. Cp. *Tg. Ps. J.* Lev. 18: 22; 20.13. For the use of the root *s-m-s,* see Marcus Jastrow,

A Dictionary of the Targumin, the Talmud Babli and Yeru-shalmi, and the Midrashic Literature (Brooklyn, NY: P. Shalom, 1967), pp. 1601-02.

[19]Marvin H. Pope's claim that the Apocrypha and Pseudepigrapha clearly supports an understanding of the sins of Sodom as homosexuality is not clearly supported by his sources; cf. Pope, *ibid.*, p. 415.

[20]F. I. Andersen, "2 (Slavonic Apocalypse of) Enoch," in *The Old Testament Pseudepigrapha*, vol. 1, edited by James H. Charlesworth (Garden City, NY: Doubleday, 1983), pp. 94-97.

[21]On Philo's attitude toward homosexuality, see P. W. van rer Horst, *The Sentences of Pseudo Phocylides* (Studia in Veretis Testimenti Pseudepigrapha, vol. 4; Leiden: Brill, 1978), pp. 111, 238; and Isaak Heinemann, *Philons griechisch und jüdische Bildung, Kulturergleichende Untersuchungen zu Philons Darstellung der Jüdische Gesetz* (Breslau: M. & M. Marcus, 1932), pp. 238f. In addition to Philo's strong positions against homosexual behavior can be found in *Ps. Phocyl.* 3, 190, 214, and in the *Sibylline Oracles*. The *Sibyl* includes homosexual relationships with boys as part of its condemnation of the Romans (*Sib. Or.* 3:182-90; 5:166, 386-97). The Jews, unlike the Gentiles, are neither idolatrous nor do they have impious intercourse with male children (*Sib. Or.* 3:595). The righteous, in general, do not commit adultery nor do they have sex with males (*Sib. Or.* 4:33-34). In the period of God's reign, there will be no more adultery or the illicit love of boys (*Sib. Or.* 5:430).

Condemnations of homosexual behavior appear clearly in early Christian literature, for example: *Barnabas* 10, as well as in certain Greco-Roman moralists, most notably: Musonius Rufus.

²²The Greek word *meixis* ("union") is translated by J.
Becker as *Vermischung*, and by Kee as "sexual relations."
Jürgen Becker, *Die Testemente der zwölf Patriarchen* (Jud-
ische Schriften aus Hellenistischromanischer Zeit, vol. 3.1;
Gütersloh: Gütersloher Verlagshaus Gerd Mohn, 1974), p.
57; Howard C. Kee, "The Testaments of the Twelve Patriarchs," *The Old Testament Pseudepigrapha* vol. 1, edited by
James H. Charlesworth (Garden City, NY: Doubleday, 1983),
p. 793.

²³Other sources that mention homosexuality (usually
pederasty) and adultery together include: *Wis.* 14:26; Philo,
Spec. Leg. II:50; *Hyp.* 7:1; Josephus, *Contra Ap.* 2:215; 1
Cor. 6:9-10; *Barn.* 19:4; *Did.* 2:2.

It seems that the association of adultery and homosexuality is to forbid any sexual activity with anyone other than
one's wife. Instructive in this regard is the *War Scroll* (1 QSM
7:3), one of the Dead Sea Scrolls, which prohibits women
and young men from entering the camps of the Israelite army
during the eschatological war. In this case, at least, both
women and young men were seen as sources of sexual entice-
ment.

The association of male-male sexual relations with a list
of forbidden heterosexual unions appears in Leviticus 18 and
20. Cf. S. F. Bigger, "The Family Laws of Leviticus 18 in
Their Setting," in *Journal of Biblical Literature* 98 (1979),
pp. 181-203. Bigger discusses the Levitical laws pertaining to
incest in light of understanding of purity regulations. Sexual
discharges in general were subject to purity regulations because of their association with the mystery of life and death
which are threatening to the stability of the social order. He
argues that homosexual relations were associated with adultery, because both involved the "misuse" of semen. Purity
language, however, does not appear in the discussion of sexual relations in *T. Naph.*

24 Helmut Koester, "Nomos Physeos, The Concept of Natural Law in Greek Thought," in *Religions in Antiquity (Essays in Memory of E. R. Goodenough)* (Leiden: Brill, 1968), pp. 512-42. As part of his condemnation of sexual relationships between men, Philo uses the expression *kata physin* ("according to nature") to describe the divinely approved unions of men and women as compared to the forbidden homosexual ones (*de Abr.*, 133-41).

25 In general, the *T. 12 Patr.* doe not appear to derive much from Hellenistic philosophy. Even if Kee is correct in seeing the influence of stoic ethics on the *T. 12 Patr.* (Howard C. Kee, "The Ethical Dimensions"), the Testaments do not exhibit the conscious application of Stoic virtues on Jewish teachings and law as, for example, does *4 Macc.* The *T. 12 Patr.* is not philosophic in the sense of the writings of Philo, or the *Wisdom of Solomon*, or even *Pseudo-Phocylides*.

26 Walter Bauer, William F. Arndt and F. Wilbur Gingrich, *A Greek-English Lexicon of the New Testament and Other Early Christian Literature* (Chicago: The University of Chicago Press, 1972), p. 869.

27 " 'paidogonos physis arsen' is a periphrasis for 'male genitals'," in P. W. van der Horst, *The Sentences of Pseudo-Phocylides*, p. 235.

28 The synoptic gospels testify to the common belief that angels are sexless. After the resurrection of the dead, it is argued that people will be like the angels in heaven who neither marry nor are married. Joseph A. Fitzmyer, *The Gospel According to Luke X-XXIV* (Anchor Bible, vol. 28A; Garden City, NY: Doubleday, 1985), 1305: *"They are like angels*: **i.e.** disembodied spirits who do not marry." See also: Philo, *Sacrif.* 1:5, Abraham, having died, became like the angels who are "unbodied and blessed souls"; *2 Apoc. Bar.*

51:10; *1 Enoch* 15:6-7, addressed to the Watchers: "indeed
you, formerly you were spiritual, [having] eternal life, and
immortal in all the generations of the world. 7. That is why
[formerly] I did not make wives for you, for the dwelling of
the spiritual beings of heaven is heaven" (translated by E.
Isaac, "I Enoch," in *The Old Testament Pseudepigrapha* vol.
1, edited by James H. Charlesworth (Garden City, NY:
Doubleday, 1983), p. 21).

[29]Translation: David Winston, *The Wisdom of Solomon*
(Anchor Bible, vol. 43; Garden City, NY: Doubleday, 1978),
p. 267.
    Marvin H. Pope argues that the context of *T. Naph.* 3:4
favors an "implicitly homosexual interpretation," finding
support in the Akkadian terminology for the change of the
servants of Ishtar from male to female (see his, "Homosexuality," p. 417). Robin Scroggs, following D. S. Bailey, *Homosexuality in the Western Christian Tradition* (New York:
Longmans, Green & Co., 1955), pp. 45-48, argues that it is a
strange and awkward expression if it refers to homosexuality.
    The parallels David Winston, *ibid*, p. 280, cites are not
particularly helpful in this matter: Philo, *Cher.* 92; *T. Naph.*
3:4; Rom. 1:26.

[30]The condemnation of the wicked priests in *T. Levi* 17:
11 supports this contention. The list of their sins closely
parallels the list of the sins of the idolaters in *Wis.* 14. Like
the Gentiles, these corrupt priests will be idolaters, quarrel-
some, money-lovers, arrogant, lawless, licentious, corrupters
of children and givers to unnatural vice with animals. See:
David Winston, *loc. cit.*

[31]Although *T. Levi* 17:11, predicts that the priesthood
of the future, the Hellenized priesthood of the Greco-Roman
period, will be guilty of a number of crimes (including the
seduction of children and bestiality) the discussion of T Naph

3:1-4.1 does not focus on the sexual abuse of male children by adult men. Rather, the concern appears to be sexual relations between adult men.

In the discussion of male-male sexual relations in rabbinic literature the age of the participants is important although it appears that the most common occurance would be relations between two adult men. While both the active and the passive partner in an act of male-male sexual intercourse are liable for punishment (*b. Sanh*. 54a), the age of the parties determine the nature of the penalty. If both were adults, they were both liable for the death penalty under Torah law. If one was an adult and the other a child of nine years and a day to thirteen, the adult was held liable for the death penalty by Torah law and the child for a flogging for disobedience by the decree of the rabbis. If one was an adult and the other a child nine years and younger, both were free from the penalty by Torah law although the adult was liable for a flogging for disobedience by the decree of the rabbis (*Sifra* on Lev. 20:13; *b. Sanh*. 54a; Rambam, *Yad,* Hilkot Genevah 1: 10; *Sefer Ha*-Chinnukh No. 209).

[32] The literature to which the teachings on sexuality in the *T. 12 Patr.* bear the closest resemblance—*Ben Sira, Wisdom of Solomon, Pseudo-Phocylides,* the "Catholic" *Epistles, Barnabas, Hermas* and the *Didache*—derive on the whole from an urban setting. The overall consistency in this teaching points to similarities in social class and family structure among the communities to whose members this instruction was addressed.

[33] Kenneth J. Dover, "Classical Greek Attitudes to Sexual Behavior," in *Women in the Ancient World: The Arethusa Papers,* ed. J. Peradotto and J. P. Sullivan (Albany, NY: State University of New York Press, 1984), p. 153.

[34] David L. Balch, *Let Wives be Submissive, The Domestic Code in 1 Peter* (SBL Monograph Series, vol. 26; Chico, CA: Scholars, 1981), pp. 54-55; *idem*, "Two Apologetic Encomia: Dionysius on Rome and Josephus on the Jews," in *Journal for the Study of Judaism* 13 (1981), pp. 102-121.

[35] The terms *paidophthoros* ("child seducer") and *ktenophthoros* ("beast seducer") appear in *T. Levi* 17:11 among a list of sinners who will appear in priestly circles in the fifth week of the seventh jubilee. John Boswell, *ibid*, pp. 41-59, 91-117. K. J. Dover, *loc. cit.*

Patriarchy, Dualism, and Homophobia:
Marginalization as Spiritual Challenge

(i) Patriarchy and Dualism

From the earliest days of the post-war women's movement in the U.S., lesbians, and later, gay men as well, have
come to realize that the very same patriarchal structures,
which are interwoven throughout the entire history of western consciousness, culture, and religion, undergird both sexism and heterosexism.   In fact, the inordinate valuing of
heterosexual men and male sexuality entered western consciousness simultaneously with the earliest beginnings of
Judaeo-Christianity.   Batya Bauman sardonically remarks
that "attributing sanctity" to male gender and sexuality is
fundamental to the "whole saga of the Jewish people," insofar as Abraham and his male god chose circumcision as the
mark of their covenant.[1] What began with Abraham and the
patriarchs of Judaism influenced Christianity, which in turn
influenced all subsequent western consciousness.   Nelle
Morton has even asserted that "compulsory heterosexuality
or homophobia ... appears to find in patriarchal religion its
foremost stronghold."[2]
  Ultimately, the human need for "ontological security,"
or meaning, developed as a need to control, especially to
control sexuality and human interrelationships.[3]   Within
Christianity it produced an ascetic spirituality utterly opposed to the body-affirming doctrine of creation. This persistent mind/body or spirit/body dualism was not a novel
concept. Christianity simply infused already dualistic Greek
ideas with a parallel set of concepts already implicit in first
century Judaism between the sacred or spiritual realm
(*ruhniut*) and the profane world of the physical (*gashmiut*).[4]
Finding its fullest expression in Christianity, this polarization
of the "self" or the spirit from the world and the body, easily

led to categorization, to the polarization of the "self" from other persons. The accompanying hierarchical values clearly placed heterosexual, ascetic (or, sexless) men over against both women and homosexuals, who were more associated with sexuality, the passions, and the irrational. Private, individual sexuality became the heart of religious doctrines of sin and salvation, while social injustice and social reformation were ignored by the status quo.[5] Ironically, patriarchy's disproportionate devaluation of human sexuality not only led it to externalize, objectivize, and empty sexuality of spiritual meaning; it also led western culture, and particularly Christianity, to become obsessed with the very sexuality it sought to stifle.

This narrow categorizing of people and behaviors which has resulted from patriarchy and dualism, the restrictions and either/ors particularly of hetero- versus homosexuality, have diminished all human sexuality and underminded the fecund energies which nurture human relationships, human love, and social justice. By making sexuality sinful, by confining sexuality to rigid gender roles, and by reducing its function solely to that of procreation, patriarchy has severed sexuality from intimate human loving. On its instrumentalist side, patriarchal sexuality ignores the problems of an overcrowded and nearly resource-exhausted world. More importantly still, it ignores the relationally enhancing power of sexuality as the expression of love and mutuality in relationships. It fails to acknowledge the possibility that human sexuality, as loving, pleasuring, humanizing, and empowering, is *intrinsically* valuable.[6]

In such a dualistic and life-denying culture, for which the inbreaking of AIDS seems only to confirm the devaluation of human bodiliness and human sexuality, it is not suprising that the challenge which homosexuality represents—toward gender roles and toward narrowly defined, life-denying and love-denying sexual behaviors—is "profoundly subversive."[7] It is also not surprising that a culture so restricted and so defended would feel compelled to bring its fullest energies to bear upon opposing and oppressing "profoundly subversive" gay men and lesbians. Indeed, the structures and dynamics of patriarchy and dualism—of sexism, heterosexism, and homophobia—together shape the context in which we experience gay oppression as the location of our theological reflection.

(ii) Homophobia and Gay Oppression

"Exile" is the word which encapsulates, for John Fortunato, the "gestalt" of gay oppression, the "constant, chronic feeling of not belonging, of being threatened and rejected," which permeates our experiences as gay men and lesbians.[8] What is especially striking about our oppression as gay people, as virtually unlike that of any other group in America today, is that the oppression of gay people is not only firmly grounded in the patriarchal structures of western consciousness; gay oppression is also religiously sanctioned and legally encouraged. Some 25 states still consider homosexuals as criminals, an opinion upheld by the 1986 Supreme Court ruling in *Bowers v. Hardwick*. This legal tyranny over the lives of gay men and lesbians stems from and is upheld by a blurring of the separation of church and state, and by the efforts of patriarchal legislators and justices to enforce a majority morality itself based upon some very poorly conceived theology. Institutionalized religion, in collusion with popular morality and governmental sanction, has encouraged "hiddenness, shame, guilt, and broken lives" among gay people, while fostering a "false respectability," a double-standard as to what is sexually tolerable outside marriage, as long as it is heterosexual.[9]

Before his death, David Goodstein also ventured to suggest that many of the problems which gay people have with being gay emerge in the spiritual struggle with the essentially religious roots of popular morality and legal restrictions, a struggle dominated by a sense of sexual shame, which results

because we assume that we are breaking biblical and traditional commandments, which we still imbue with authority,
and not just secular laws. This shame maintains our closets
and paralyzes our capacity for action. In collusion with our
gay ghettoization, the biblical authority and shame structure,
when still accepted at *any* level by us, perpetuates itself and
enables both religious and civil oppressors to retain their
power over us.[10]

John Fortunato asserts that oppression is simply "what
gay people face when they are authentic," when they are
honest with themselves and, certainly, when they are honest
with others.[11] Early in the process of gay self-awareness,
oppression includes self-denial, religious doubt, and the consequent guilt and senses of unworthiness, loneliness, and fear
of disclosure. Once an individual is identifiable as gay, oppression broadens to encompass a wide range of experiences,
including the potential loss of a job or the denial of one's
right to practice his/her profession, and any consequent
financial frustrations. Job security and hope for advance-
ment dissolve as one is ignored, passed over, or worse, never
even allowed admittance to the professional system (as with
the church). Gerre Goodman and co-authors, for example,
have argued that "jobs that are available to [open] lesbians
and gays are primarily blue collar or service-oriented. Middle-
and upper-class jobs are not easily available to *openly* gay
people."[12] Similarly, John Fortunato goes so far as to
speculate that *openly* gay people "fall into the lowest national income categories."[13] The combination of sexism and
homophobia clearly consigns a large percentage of gay men
at least to jobs which have traditionally been reserved for
women; the gay men in such jobs are, accordingly, devalued
and paid *as women* and not as "real" competitive and pro-
ductive males. The myth of "gay disposable income" is just
that, the privilege of a minority of (frequently closeted,
white) gay men.

In addition to impaired economic survival, and unlike

other minorities, openly gay people often experience rejection and avoidance by their families, which in turn encourages gay ghettoization. Even in the relative "safety in numbers" of an urban gay ghetto, however, gay oppression still includes incidents of verbal and physical anti-gay violence and the absence of secular or ecclesiastical protections. Gay people enjoy no legal protections, making any public display of affection acceptable for heterosexuals utterly taboo for gay people, gay aliens may be denied entry into the U.S.; gay parents may lose not only custody of, but even visitation rights to, their children; and, all gay people are subject to police harassment and, when anti-gay crimes are reported, often find themselves punished and their attacker(s) set free. In addition, gay and lesbian couples enjoy *no* legal or financial benefits, no social support, no tax breaks, no spousal insurance benefits, and no public ceremonies to hallow our relationships. Gay partners cannot "marry," "divorce," or bequeath with any assurances. Same sex couples may even experience difficulties in finding housing or tolerant landlords. In a society which so stresses the value of heterosexual nuclear families, and which simultaneously condemns so-called gay promiscuity, this lack of support for, and sometimes outright hostility toward, gay couples or gay "surrogate families," is especially reprehensible.

As a people exiled on the margins, gay men and lesbians are forced into the frustrating position of trying to nurture and sustain self-worth and self-esteem while confronted with both religious condemnation and the absence of legal protections and social structures. We must learn to love ourselves and others "in the face of utter rejection" by a society steeped in heterosexual (and usually white, male) values.[14] Simply by virture of being gay, we must not only give up attachment to what might have been but wasn't; we must also let go of what the present and the future might have held but now will not. This constant state of embattlement by a surrounding, homophobic society feeds self-denigration and internalized

oppression. The constant losses and constant fear are "wearing, draining, and demoralizing."[15]   Or, as Larry Uhrig has
said, "that gay people must expend greater energy to accom-
plish traditional goals [in the face of so many obstacles] is a
constant drain upon energies which could be directed toward
the achievement of other goals badly needed by our society,
our communities, and ourselves."[16]

The clear result of these combined forces is that long ago
gay people, our lives, and our particular talents went under-
ground. A community in exile shaped a subculture whose
temples, town halls and social clubs became the gay bars and
the realm of the night, where gay people could dare to gather
together for fellowship, mutual support, and loving sexuality.
Two brief decades of above-ground, daylit gay liberation have
not displaced this particular center of our communal being;
while we are increasingly open and visible throughout society
and in the struggles both for gay rights and for an adequate
political, social, and medical response to AIDS, we still carry
with us not only the memories but also the present realities
of oppression. Many gay people are still ghettoized in urban
neighborhoods and our subculture is still very much shaped
by and consigned to spaces and times which are nonthreaten-
ing to our heterosexist oppressors.

Homophobia in church and state has shaped not only the
gay subculture, but gay self-understandings and behaviors as
well. Of particular concern, for example, is the impact of
homophobia and ghettoization upon gay relationships. While
a consistent theme in the writings of Edward Carpenter[17]
and Harry Hay[18] or throughout the poetry of Walt Whitman[19] suggests that by lying between the opposites, gay
people *can* be more relational, mutual, democratic, and androgynous, real ghettoized gay life often remains hierarchical
and exclusive. Mirroring the patriarchy which circumscribes
it, the gay subculture, among gay men at least, has frequently
created its own hierarchies of economic status, race, age, sexual style, and appearance. Rather than actually embodying

the ideal possibilities of mutually subjective relating, the sexually focused gay bar subculture, shaped as it has been by heterosexual values and the heterosexual need to control and bracket gay people, has often actually undercut gay mutuality. Gay men, at least, have too often sustained the love/sex dichotomy and treated both self and others solely as sexual objects ... until AIDS.[20]

Such self-criticism, however, must be grounded not in self-blaming, but in compassionate reflection and action. Our community's response to AIDS, for example, has taught us that we can transform gay baths into health centers and gay bars into gathering places which are more socially and communally mutual, and less sexually objectifying. We can recognize our need for gay spaces on the margins of heterosexual acceptability as the physical location both of our celebrations of gay life and of our launching our liberation struggles, as from the Stonewall Inn in 1969. Moreover, we can reflectively penetrate the patriarchal structures which maintain our ghettoization and relearn to nurture non-competitive and non-self-loathing gay mutuality.

(iii) Oppression and Gay Spirituality

John Fortunato further indicates that by going through our senses of oppression, grief, and anger—by going deeper—we can ultimately discover and touch our spiritual grounding, our wellspring of compassion, empathy, and empowerment. We must grieve both the trivial and the not-so-trivial losses, all those situations and opportunities in the past, present and the future which have been and are and will be denied to us, simply because we are gay. Once we are able to push past our suffering, to touch and express our anger, to grieve our losses, and to realize that, as gay people, we have no secured future, we may then discover that God's presence is revealed not in heterosexual acceptability, but in the depths both of grieving gay losses and of transcending oppression here and now, in order to embrace our outcast status ... our exile.[21]

By "taking life as it comes," by confronting and not denying the "pain that life includes," and by doing our grief work, we are freed to move on.[22] We can discover God's presence in both our anger and our grief; we can use our very experience of oppression to deepen our spirituality; and through this process, we can discover both the spiritual and communal empowerment for moving on, for living in what Carter Heyward calls "radical participation" in the present processes of liberation.[23] Working through our sense of oppression enables us not only to revalue and to accept our good gay and lesbian selves and our sexuality, in the present; it also enables us to reclaim our personal (and our corporate) past, retrospectively accepting the givens of our lives and *choosing* to relinquish those things from which we are and will be excluded. According to John Fortunato, moving from passive victimization to an assertive, self-emptying place on the margins can open us to both the inner peace and the rightfulness of our place in the cosmos and with God. Gay men and lesbians can transcend oppression by confronting and not denying our losses; we can be empowered by the energies of grief *and* anger to claim God's presence in our midst, to celebrate our gay selves, and to struggle together for justice.[24]

From the deeper and broader self-acceptance and our deepened spirituality, gained through confronting gay oppression, we can learn indeed that "the God of the bible ... is biased in favor of the [oppressed]."[25] We learn that *all* of creation, with all its great diversity, including homosexuality, is good. We also learn to be aware of and to assume appropriate responsibility for roles which we assume under homophobia; and, in "naming the demons," we are able to set aside those roles, to be freed from them. So freed and empowered, by God's companionship with us and advocacy for us at the margins, we are also able to develop a more *in*clusive compassion not only for ourselves and for one another, but for other marginalized and struggling people, and ultimately even for our oppressors. We can also exercise our creativity and our greater willingness to risk experimenting with life options otherwise precluded by patriarchy and heterosexism. We can nurture our deepened spirituality and meaning systems and insist upon celebrating life and human sexuality in the very midst of rejection, suffering, and oppression. We can create our own defiant wholeness and, from our grounding in cosmic self-acceptance, tap the energies needed to fuel our quest for justice.[26]

However, there is one more wrinkle in the fabric of our experiences of gay life and gay oppression. There is one more challenge to our efforts to analyze our oppression and to develop psychological and spiritual wholeness. AIDS. A virus which is blind to right or wrong, to goodness or badness, and to gender or sexual orientation. And our homophobic and heterosexist culture has responded to AIDS by coming down harder still upon the gay community. The reality of AIDS suffering, death, and grief in our community, coupled with renewed homophobia and anti-gay violence, places everything we do in a different perspective. It adds another layer to our oppression text and it will shape our theology in ways which will differ from feminist and other liberation theologies. Our particular minority experience of human injustice is further complicated by the random cruelty of the cosmos and our realization of God's limitations in tragedy.

(iv) AIDS and Redoubled Oppression

The link in western religious thought between sexuality as the heart of sinfulness and sinfulness as the cause of human mortality, as a divine punishment for sexual "sin," has widened the gulf between sexuality and spirituality and thus further damned those people who insist upon being sexual. To be sexual, according to this tradition, particularly in non-heterosexual and non-procreative ways, is to choose bodiliness, sinfulness, mortality, and death over the "higher" values of eternal, spiritual life. Gay people, by being sexual, sexually different, and even unmonogamously and unrigidly sexual, are naturally seen by our dualistic tradition as the most arrogant rejectors of "higher spirituality" and thus already as corrupt death-bringers, a view strongly reinforced by AIDS devastation in our particular community. In the present tragedy of AIDS, this tradition of dualism and hierarchical values (of eternal spirituality vs. sexuality and bodiliness) blames those who are suffering and dying of AIDS for their dilemma. Patriarchy's "real sin," however, is manifest in the vicious circle whereby the social and religious condemnation of gay people, particularly gay men, has historically so undermined gay self-esteem and self-worth as to compel many of us to seek personal confirmation in excessive or even compulsive sexual gratification, which in turn placed us increasingly at risk for AIDS and hence at risk for further social and religious condemnation.[27]

John Fortunato emphasizes the numerous fears which AIDS adds to our experience of gay oppression, particularly for gay men now and in the immediate future—our fear of already having AIDS as we await symptoms to appear or a diagnosis to be pronounced; our fears regarding the uncertainty of AIDS-related complex (ARC); our fears about the physical process of AIDS itself; our constant grief and fear and guilt as survivors, and as survivors who might have passed the virus to our friends, lovers, and partners in the early years before we understood safe-sex practices; and, finally, our fear of AIDS-phobic hatred and increased anti-gay violence.[28] The mixture, then, of AIDS-phobia and homophobia in the popular consciousness not only confronts gay men with the very real prospect of having to adjust to a terminal condition at some not too distant point; it also revives all the pain of the process of self-discovery, self-acceptance, and self-closure.[29]

According to Leon Howell, the practical ramifications of combined AIDS-phobia and homophobia are such that "many of those with AIDS lose their jobs, their friends, their lovers, their living quarters, their insurance, and, in a number of cases, medical care and preparation of their bodies for burial."[30] They may also experience further isolation from or utter rejection by their families, as they are abandoned to die among strangers; or conversely, they may discover that their well-meaning families have excluded their gay friends and lovers from access to the processes of caring and grieving for them. Gay people-with-AIDS (PWAs) are confronted both by this irrational, victim-blaming behavior toward them and by their own self-blaming, whenever they accept the social and religious condemnations of their sexuality, and of their very value as human beings, while they are simultaneously confronted by the pain and physical wasting of each new opportunistic infection, by the pain and discomfort of medical treatments, and by the ultimate terminality of AIDS.

For those of us who are as yet survivors, our fears and uncertainties, our grief and guilt, are further complicated. To our fears regarding our own exposure is the added pain of hearing, often weekly, of another friend who has been diagnosed or who has died. In our twenties, thirties, and forties we are constantly confronted with the ongoing loss of our peers, an experience more developmentally appropriate for adults seventy or older, or for men in combat. And, when we lose friends or even a lover, our grief itself is often frustrated. Because our sexuality is outlawed and our relationships unprotected by law, we often have no forum for our grief. We are frequently excluded from the funerals of our loved ones by families who are themselves struggling, perhaps for the very first time, with both a son's homosexuality and a son's AIDS. Because in the popular consciousness an AIDS diagnosis is virtually a declaration of homosexuality, families and newspapers hide the cause of death with euphemisms; we cannot even claim our dead in order to mourn them. And, finally, an alarming number of Americans favor quarantine or internment for people-with-AIDS (PWAs), for people-with-ARC (PWARCs), for HIV carriers (the HIV virus is the putative cause of AIDS), and even for persons "merely suspect" (all gay men, for example). And of course, such isolation would be life-long, because HIV infection and certainly "mere suspicion" remain incurable.[31]

Even in the gloom of AIDS-redoubled gay oppression, however, the possibility of spiritual deepening nevertheless remains alive for us. AIDS has shaped the gay and lesbian community into a people of increasing compassion, of response and caring. The gay communities, both gay men and lesbians, were the first to form agencies to minister to the sick, the first to lobby for increased funding for AIDS research and care, and the first to teach pastors and churches how to care, how to minister to people-with-AIDS and people-with-ARC. AIDS is focusing for us a theologizing which *is* our praxis, strengthening our thirst for justice and sharpening our rage at the heartless ones who claim AIDS is God's punishment and who are happy at gay deaths.[32] AIDS has, for example, clarified our need and our demand to bless and sanctify gay couplings as redemptive, nurturant, intrinsically good relationships and *not merely* as convenient, monogamous forms of disease control.[33] AIDS has also underscored the need to nurture gay spirituality and to develop a gay liberation theology which affirms and celebrates the plurality and variety of God's creation, including the full spectrum of human sexuality, as good.

AIDS has clearly forced us to raise significant questions for the activity of theology: How, for example, can we stay in touch with our sexual power-in-relationship, or in community, in the face of AIDS? Has AIDS, or increased monogamous coupling, or "safe sex" changed or diminished our sexual power? Can we love one another and celebrate our sexuality and reclaim the bonding power, the prophetically motivating power, of our sexuality, amidst AIDS, AIDS-phobia, and homophobia? Can we still, *can we again*, insist upon the unqualified, intrinsic goodness of non-procreative sexuality as the expression and source of love, pleasure, empowerment, and God's co-delight, over against the hatred and judgment which AIDS has evoked? It is especially crucial, now more than ever, that we do so! In fact, our very raising of these and other questions and our beginning, however partially, to respond theologically to these questions as well as to care for our suffering friends, together constitute the birth of that activity which can become a gay liberational reconstruction of Judaeo-Christian theology.

—**J. Michael Clark, Ph.D.**

NOTES

[1] Batya Bauman, "Women-identified women in male-identified Judaism," in *On being a Jewish feminist: A reader* (ed. S. Heschel, New York: Schocken Books, 1983), p. 91.

[2] Nelle Morton, *The journey is home* (Beacon: Beacon Press, 1985), p. xxx.

[3] Mitch Walker, *Visionary love: A spiritbook of gay mythology & transmutational faerie* (San Francisco: Treeroots Press, 1980), p. 16, cf. pp. 17, 22.

[4] Judith Plaskow, "The right question is theological," in *On being a Jewish feminist: A reader* (ed. S. Heschel; New York: Schocken Books, 1983), p. 225.

[5] cf., Rosemary Radford Ruether's discussion of the displacement of social justice by concepts of privatized sin/salvation in her *Liberation theology* (New York: Paulist Press, 1972), especially pp. 17-18.

[6] Ara Doustourian, "Gayness: A radical Christian approach," in *The gay academic* (ed. L. Crew; Palm Springs: Etc. Publications, 1978), pp. 336-337f.

[7] Gerre Goodman, *et al., No turning back: Lesbian & gay liberation for the '80s* (Philadelphia: New Society Publishers, 1983), p. 36.

[8] John E. Fortunato, *Embracing the exile: Healing journeys of gay Christians* (New York: Seabury Press, 1983), p. 86.

[9] Malcolm Boyd, *Take off the masks* (Philadelphia: New Society Publishers, 1984), pp. 81, 92, 120.

[10] David Goodstein, "Opening space [editorial]," *The Advocate,* no. 414 (19 February 1985), p. 6.

[11] Fortunato, *ibid.*, p. 87.

[12] Goodman, *et al., ibid.*, p. 43 (emphasis added).

[13] Fortunato, *ibid.*, p. 81.

[14] *Ibid.*, p. 18.

[15] Goodman, *et al., ibid.*, p. 13.

[16] Larry J. Uhrig, *The two of us: Affirming, celebrating, and symbolizing gay & lesbian relationships* (Boston: Alyson Publications, 1984), p. 101.

[17] Edward Carpenter, "On the connexion between homosexuality and divination," in *Revue d'Ethnographie et de Sociologie*, vol. 11-12 (1910), pp. 301-316, and *Intermediate types among primitive folk* (2d ed.; London: Allen & Unwin,

1919 [photo reprint; New York: Arno Press, 1975]).

[18] Harry Hay, "A separate people whose time has come," in *Gay spirit: Myth & Meaning* (ed. M. Thompson; New York: St. Martin's Press, 1987), pp. 279-291.

[19] cf., W. Moritz, "Seven glimpses of Walt Whitman," in *Gay spirit: Myth & Meaning* (ed. M. Thompson; New York: St. Martin's Press, 1987), pp. 131-151.

[20] Hay, *ibid.*, p. 288.

[21] cf., Fortunato, *loc. cit.*.

[22] *Ibid.*, pp. 56, 107.

[23] I. Carter Heyward, *Our passion for justice: Images of power, sexuality, & liberation* (New York: Pilgrim Press, 1984), p. 68.

[24] cf. Fortunato, *loc. cit.*

[25] Matthew Fox, "The spiritual journey of the homosexual ... & just about everyone else," in *A challenge to love: Gay & lesbian Catholics in the church* (ed. R. Nugent; New York: Crossroad/Continuum, 1983), p. 195.

[26] C. J. Topper, "Spirituality as a component in counseling lesbian-gays," in *Journal of Pastoral Counseling* 21.1 (Spring-Summer 1986), pp. 55-59.

[27] E. E. Shelp, R. H. Sunderland, & P. W. A. Mansell, *AIDS: Personal stories in pastoral perspective* (New York: Pilgrim Press, 1986), pp. 63, 94.

[28] John E. Fortunato, "AIDS: The plague that lays waste

at noon," in *The Witness* 68.9 (September 1985), pp. 6-9.

²⁹B. J. Stiles, "AIDS and the churches," in *Christianity & Crisis* 45.22 ([January] 1986), pp. 534-536.

³⁰Leon Howell, "Churches and AIDS: Responsibilities in mission," in *Christianity & Crisis* 45.20 ([December] 1985), p. 483.

³¹C. Rowland, "The call for quarantine," *The Advocate* no. 443 (1986), pp. 42-46.

³²cf., J. Michael Clark, "AIDS, death & God: Gay liberational theology & the problem of suffering," in *Journal of Pastoral Counseling* 21.1 (Spring-Summer 1986), pp. 40-54, and "Special considerations in pastoral care of gay persons-with-AIDS," in *Journal of Pastoral Counseling* 22.1 (Spring-Summer 1987), pp. 32-45.

³³Fortunato, "AIDS: The plague that lays waste at noon," p. 9.

SOCIAL/SCIENTIFIC ANALYSIS

"In this section the contribution on both Nazi and post-war German social and legal policies toward gays examines the effects of a racist and national-populist sexual morality in recent world history. Theological and ethical implications of contemporary homophobic violence are presented in the second paper. The point developed from historical overview and empirical data is that the attacked form movements of solidarity in response to encountered violence. Therewith, greater visibility is achieved and the 'strangers' are enabled to a more effective position within society."

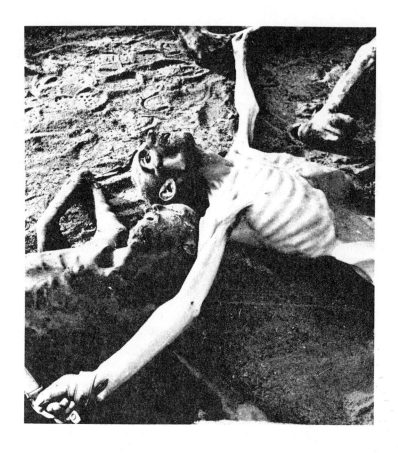

German concentration camps—the dead and the dying as found by Western armies in 1945. The Nazis set up their first concentration camps in Germany to hold the German opponents of their regime, but later, after the war had begun and had moved east into non-German territory, the new camps established in Poland were deliberately planned as part of Hitler's "final solution," the extermination of the Jews, although Jews were not his only victims. Even in those camps not avowedly dedicated to extermination the conditions were brutal in the extreme,

Gays—A Threat to Society?
Social Policy in Nazi Germany and the Aftermath

(i) Introduction

Gays, along with gypsies and Jehovah's Witnesses, belong to the forgotten victims of the Nazi terror. They did not fit into the ideological mold of the Nazi regime whose ideals were 'state,' 'family,' and 'Mother-Cross.' Lacking the ability, according to Nazi philosophy, to contribute in any positive way to the state, the easiest way to deal with them was to annihilate them. By extending Nazi legislation into its Penal Code, the Federal Republic of Germany accepted the persecution and physical annihilation of homosexuals during the Third Reich as perfectly legal and morally unobjectionable. The German Democratic Republic, on the other hand, excelled quite early through tolerant jurisprudential practice. General social acceptance of gay people, however, continued to limp behind legal practice.

Gays are forgotten victims because, although they were victimized by the thousands during the Third Reich, they were not recognized as victims neither by the successor state to the Third Reich, today's Federal Republic of Germany, nor by the German Democratic Republic. The secular regimes in the two German countries did not ascribe victim status to gays persecuted by the Nazis. Organized religion of the Protestant and Catholic variety did its best not to make the questions of restitution and retribution to persecuted homosexuals a matter of political concern, mainly by remaining quiet about the issue.

Many victims who had survived the Nazi terror were, at first, unable to speak or write about their ordeal during the twelve years of the Third Reich. Eventually, however, they wrote down what they had experienced, either in the autobiographical genre or as quasi-autobiographical fiction (*e.g.*:

Elle Wiesel's *Night* (originally published in Paris, 1958).

The gay victims of the Nazi terror could not do this for almost three decades lest they publicly affirm themselves as homosexuals in the socio-political environment at least of the Federal Republic of Germany. The Federal Republic continued to criminalize homosexual activities among consenting adults until 1973. Perhaps the best known account of a gay victim of the Nazis is Heinz Heger's *Die Menner mit dem rosa Winkel* [1] which was published in America under the title *The Men with the Pink Triangle*. A quotation from the English edition:

> *Thousands upon thousands of homosexuals must have lost their tormented lives there, victims of a deliberate operation of destruction by the Hitler regime. And yet till this very day no one has come forward to describe this and honour its victims. It seems that 'good taste' nowadays prevents people from speaking of the destruction of concentration-camp victims, particularly when these were homosexuals.* [2]

There are but a few scholarly investigations into the life and suffering of homosexuals during the Third Reich. [3] Autobiographical accounts as well as research works have, unfortunately, not enjoyed wide reception. Autobiographical accounts deal largely with the actual situation and living conditions of gays in Nazi prisons and concentration camps. Generally speaking, they present material about homosexuals in the time when *gay*-nocide was already a *fait accompli* in Nazi politics. Only a few scholarly works give exact information about how the Nazis from their early days in the 1920s and after their seizure of absolute political power in 1933 followed a hard line against gays and homosexuality in German society. The hard line was even more emphasized after the Blood Purge against SA-Chief Ernst Roehm and his companions on June 30, 1934.

Two questions have to be answered: (1) Did the Nazis rely upon a "scientific rationale" for their policy of persecution of homosexuals, and, if so, what were the bases for such reasoning? (2) What was the actual policy implemented against gays?

Ad 1: Homosexuality and homosexual behavior were incompatible with Nazi ideology which favored such "traditional" values as state and family. And, although a whole cult was developed around the woman as mother, with increasing honors and the bestowing of badges for especially fertile members of the species, sexuality, or at least its purely physical aspects, was generally seen as something negative, however hard to define. The only reason for its existence was its necessity for procreation and, therewith, the implementation of the Empire of a Thousand Years as well as the physical manifestation of the Germanic race as superior to all other races. Sexuality within the context of the family was, at least in the early years of the Nazi reign, in a purely pragmatic way instrumental for the success of the Nazi ideology through the sheer number of adherents to the movement.

It is not difficult to see that homosexuals did not fit this ideology. From the Nazi point of view they were ballast, useless for the state, useless for the successful survival of an ideology through physical procreation. As something like a "third sex," they did neither resemble the ideal of the male as the strong Nordic warrior nor the Nazi ideal of the submissive woman whose prime vocation in life was her service to the nation through motherhood: kitchen, cult and children revisited.

The stereotypical image of the male homosexual as the perverted amalgam of both human sexes, neither a strong war hero nor a submissive "mother-machine," who, in addition, might live his sexuality purely for personal pleasure including a good dose of lust, was repulsive to Nazi ideology. Sexuality and sexual activity which was not for the greater good of the state had to be rejected. So it came that homosexuals became strangers in their own society: psycho-medically regarded as mentally ill, socially ostracized as perverse and legally in any case persecuted as criminals. They were criminals because if they had chosen to be sexually active they had come into permanent conflict with Paragraph 175 of the German Penal Code of 1871.

Nobody knows the exact number of how many gay men were killed in the Concentration Camps. Numbers range somewhere between 5,000 and 15,000.[4] It has to be taken into consideration, however, that this is only the number of gays who perished behind the barbed wire fences of Concentration Camps. But by far not all sentenced homosexuals were shipped off to Concentration Camps.

The total number of males convicted of homosexuality between 1933 and 1944[5] lies somewhere between 50,000 and 63,000.[6] The majority of them served their time within the regular prison system until the end of the war. The Concentration Camps themselves held only about 1,000 gays captive at any given time after 1935. The number was somewhat lower between 1933 and 1935.[7] This can be explained with the intensification of the rounding up of homosexuals after the "Blood Purge" of 1934 and the subsequent modifications of the anti-gay paragraph 175 of the German Penal Code.

Ad 2: Concerning the implementation of the Nazis policy against gays the available source material tends to be autobiographical.

There was no Wannsee Conference[8] with regard to the fate of homosexuals in the German Reich. No "final solution" was decided upon in a formal way. Reality, however, looked different. There was an unwritten Nazi policy of annihilation of homosexuals through labor. Labor was the only possibility by the help of which gays could be forged into useful elements for the Reich even after they had been denied all other social usefulness.

Autobiographical sources describe the actual living conditions in concentration camps as experienced by gays. Their status as convicted criminals on the one hand and, according to Nazi ideology, as "psycho-medico-biologically perverted corruptors of the morals of the German youths" on the other made them doubly vulnerable within the social hierarchy of the Concentration Camps. Incarcerated gays had to fear both the hatred of their fellow inmates and the blows of the SS-guards. The personal accounts are as informative as they are shocking. And since they deal almost exclusively with the life in the camps, they neglect to look for an analysis of the conditions of contingency for the predicament.

In order to provide a detailed answer to the second question, one has to take a look at the time before 1933 and the work of various groups in the organized scientific fight against Paragraph 175 of the German Penal Code of 1871.

(ii) Gays in the Weimar Republic: The "Wissenshaftlich-Humanitaere Komites" (Scientific Humanitarian Committee = SHC) and the Organized Struggle Against Paragraph 175 of the German Penal Code of 1871

During the time of the Weimar Republic gays in Germany were able to live reasonably well without great fear. Especially in big cities such as Munich and Berlin, it was possible to live any gay lifestyle the individual wanted to pursue. The Berlin of the 1920s was the focal point for gays as well as lesbians, because the sheer size of the city provided enough cover for a peaceful existence in the face of Paragraph 175. It was a time of great freedom—political and sexual—and people tried to live their life styles as uninhibited as possible. Thomas Lechie Jarman, who evaluated the Germany of the roaring twenties in his book *The Rise and Fall of Nazi Germany* wrote:

Freedom degenerated into license; youth en-

joyed the sunshine while it could. Bars for homosexuals, cafes where men danced with men, a new liberty between the sexes, nudism, camping, sun-bathing, pornographic literature in the corner-kiosks—all these things were accepted as part of the new life.[10]

But it was also in Berlin where serious attempts were made to fight for the complete emancipation of homosexuals in society. This was largely done through an organized fight against Paragraph 175 of the German Penal Code. Three groups who worked in that direction have to be pointed out:

1. the "Bund fuer Menschenrechte" (Union for Human Rights.

2. The "Wissenschaftlich-Humanitaere Komitee" (Scientific Humanitarian Committee) founded in 1897 by the physician Magnus Hirschfeld, and

3. the "World League for Sexual Reform" which worked closely together with the Institute of Sexual Science in Berlin (another foundation of Magnus Hirschfeld).

Of the three groups the work of the Scientific Humanitarian Committee is best documented.

Magnus Hirschfeld ranked on the absolutely lowest level in the Nazi evaluation of human beings. He was not only suspect as a scholar, but he was also a homosexual, a transvestite, and a Jew; in other words, completely unacceptable.

As early as 1898—one year after the Committee was founded—Hirschfeld wrote a petition to the German Reichstag (or parliament) asking it to do everything in its power to delete Paragraph 175 from the Penal Code. The English translation of the text of the Paragraph is as follows:

> *175. Unnatural lustful intercourse committed*
> *between males or between human beings and*
> *animals shall be punished by imprisonment;*
> *loss of civic rights may also be imposed.*[11]

Hirschfeld requested in his petition that "all sexual acts between persons of the same sex, similar to the acts between persons of the opposite sex (homosexuals and heterosexuals alike) should only be punished if they [*i.e.*, the acts] were executed under application of violence, if done to persons under 16 years of age, or if they were practiced in a way that caused 'public scandal' (*i.e.*, in violation of Paragraph 183 of the Penal Code of the German Reich)."[12]

The petition received parliamentary support from August Bebel and the deputies of the Social Democratic Party in the Reichstag, and a single vote from a National Liberal deputy. The representatives of all other parties were outraged and appalled by the contents of the petition. Hirschfeld's petition was rejected.

The Conservatives reacted to this reform attempt by means of introducing a draft of Penal Code 1909 which disregarded all previous attempts to reform Paragraph 175. They tried to extend the range of the Paragraph, so that it could also be used to criminalize female homosexual behavior. The indirectly positive result of this reactionary attempt, however was the concession of an independent sexuality of women. So far this had not played a role in the legal discussion.

Whereas before women were seen as asexual beings who could only participate through marriage in the sexuality of their husbands, women were now regarded as human beings endowed with their own sexuality and also capable of (mis)-using this precious gift. Therefore, homosexual women, like their male counterparts, should legally be held accountable for their misdoings.

The SHC was able to stop the extension of Paragraph 175 to lesbian relationships. The attempt to extend the range of

Paragraph 175 to lesbian relationships has to be seen together with the newly established emancipation movement of women in Germany. Women did not yet have the right to vote. Since the turn of the century they presented themselves, however, increasingly as a political and social force those in power would eventually have to reckon with.

In the 1920s there was even a broad discussion about the possibility of forming an independent national homosexual political party. Article 17 of the constitution of the Weimar Republic allowed the establishing of a political party if the applicants were able to muster 60,000 votes and to seat a representative in the Reichstag.

The year 1925 brought about the first official draft reform of the Penal Code. The part of the draft dealing with the reform of the sexual penal code was quite a surprise to many in the homosexual liberation movement. A counterdraft was developed by the SHC in 1927 which called for the renunciation of all laws criminalizing homosexual activity between men. The German Communist Party supported the counter-draft when it gained a seat in the Reichstag's Committe for the Reform of the Penal Code in 1929. The Communist deputy on the Committee joined the delegates of the Social Democratic Party and the German Democratic Party in their votes for the abolition of Paragraph 175. On October 16, 1929, the committee voted 15 to 13 for the decriminalization of homosexual acts between consenting adults in private.

Unfortunately, the Penal Code Reform Bill of 1929 did not make it through the full assembly of the Reichstag. Stock market crash and subsequent global economic depression turned the attention of politicians to other matters than the decriminalization of homosexuality. A great opportunity was lost here. The Nazis, who at that time were already marching in the streets in their brown uniforms promoting their simple creed of "Fuehrer," "Volk" and "blood and soil," could simply pick up what was already legally available.

They turned Paragraph 175 of the Penal Code of the Weimar Republic from a largely unenforced law into a handy political means of persecution of an undesirable group within society. In addition, they did not shy away from using the paragraph for denunciatory purposes if they saw it fit their political ends.

In all this organized religion remained extremely silent. None of the sources say anything about possible reactions of the leaders of the Catholic and Protestant Churches in Germany to the various emancipatory reform attempts of the Penal Code. It seems, however, that organized religion silently supported the position of the dominant majority concerning the illegality and immorality of homosexual activity. A genitalia-centered sexual morality sees the rightful place for human sexual activity in the matrimonial state. The procreation of the species is, with varying emphasis, promoted as the rightful end of sexual activity. This type of sexual morality cannot agree to any libertarianism concerning human sexual encounters, not to talk about the decriminalization of same sex relationships and sexual activity. The interpretation of natural law with its origin in God seemed to prohibit such a stance.

(iii) The ideology of the Nazi Party: Homosexuality as an Attack on the "Voelkisch" (national/populist) Moral Code

The Nazi Party's programs of 1920 and 1927 make no reference to homosexuality. The program of German facism concerning politics of race and population was very much directed toward marital procreative sexuality under so called "race hygienic" assumptions. It was aimed at the political interests of the future *voelkisch* (national/populist) state that a special notion of homosexuality seemed to be out of place.

It was in 1928 in a letter answering the questions of a gay

political activist by the name of Adolph Brand that the Nazi Party expressed its view concerning Paragraph 175 in unambiguous terms:

Munich, May 14, 1928

Suprema lex salus populi! *Community before individual!*

It is not necessary that you and I live, but it is necessary that the German people live. And it can live only if it can fight, for life means fighting. And it can only fight if it maintains its masculinity. It can only maintain its masculinity if it exercises discipline, especially in matters of love. Free love and deviance are undisciplined. Therefore we reject you, as we reject anything which hurts our people. Anyone who even thinks of homosexual love is our enemy. We reject anything which emasculates our people and makes it a plaything for our enemies, for we know that life is a fight and it is madness to think that men will ever embrace fraternally. Natural history teaches us the opposite. Might makes right. And the stronger will always win over the weak. Let's see to it that we once again become the strong! But this we can only do in one way—the German people must once again learn how to exercise discipline. We therefore reject any form of lewdness, especially homosexuality, because it robs us of our last chance to free our people from the bondage which now enslaves it.[13]

The language of the statement should serve as a clear warning signal to all homosexuals who favored the Nazi Party in its early years until Hitler's seizure of power in 1933 and the Roehm Purge of 1934. Two points of the statement need additional comments.

(1) "The stronger will win over the weak!" This social-Darwinistic idea fits excellently into the ideology of the Nazis. Homosexuality was seen as a perversion of human nature and homosexual activity as the pursuit of a decadent lifestyle. All decadent lifestyles would eventually vanish because they were too weak to defend themselves. They would be overcome by the stronger and hardier form of living of the new Germanic-Nordic superman. But since decadent lifestyles might not disappear fast enough it was only right to enhance the process of disappearance.

(2) "Homosexuality enslaves society!" Homosexuality, although just judged as weak was on the other hand seen as possessing a certain power. But for the Nazis this power was ill-directed and, therefore, turned out to be a threat to their ideology. Homosexuals were not useful for society. They did not help increase the German population. They did not fit the "Mother-Cross"-ideology of the upcoming Third Reich. Homosexuality had the most extreme position on the "immoral" scale of free love acts. Since procreation was excluded from their sexual acts, gays lacked "natural purpose." They did not serve the Reich but only themselves. This form of freedom was intolerable for Nazi ideology. It became therefore the main catalyst for the persecution of gays in Nazi Germany.

It is interesting to note the combination of anti-gay and anti-Jewish sentiment in ideological statements of the Nazis. An article published in the *Voelkische Beobachter*, the Nazi daily newspaper, of August 2, 1930, associates homosexuality and Jewish faith in their joint attempt to overpower Nazi ideology. In response to the 1929 decision of the Committee for the Reform of the Penal Code the *Voelkische Beobachter* wrote:

> *We congratulate you on this success, Mr. Kahl
> and Mr. Hirschfeld! But please don't believe
> that we Germans will leave these kinds of laws
> in effect for a single day, after we will have
> gained power. .... All these evil instincts of
> the Jewish soul which intend to cross the
> divine thought of creation by physical relation-
> ships to animals, to brothers and sisters, and to
> people of the same sex, we will in short terms
> mark by means of law as what they are: ter-
> rible and vulgar aberrations of Syrians, the very
> worst crime which is to be punished with the
> gallows or with expulsion.*

Another Nazi paper, the SS weekly *Das Schwarze Korps*
called vehemently for the total extermination of homosexuals. In its March 4, 1937, edition it estimated the gay population in Germany to be about 2 million, which was most likely
a gross underestimation. What the paper wanted to indicate,
however, was that these 2 million men were of no social benefit for the Reich.

The best idea about a leading Nazi's thought concerning
the problem of homosexuality and the possible solution to
the problem can be found in a passage of a speech given by
Heinrich Himmler to SS group leaders on February 18, 1937,
almost three years after the Roehm Purge and two years after
Paragraph 175 was amended:

> *We have to be clear about that if we are going
> to have this vice any longer in Germany with-
> out being able to fight it, then this will be the
> end of Germany, the end of the Germanic
> world. Unfortunately, we do not have it as easy
> as our ancestors. They only had a few individu-
> al cases of this abnormal kind. The homosexual
> man...was drowned in the marshes. That was*

*not punishment, but a simple eradication of
this abnornmal being. They had to be done
away with, as we tear out nettles, throw them
on a heap, and burn them. That was not a feeling of vengeance, but those it concerned had to
be put out of the way. That was the custom of
our ancestors. Unfortunately, I have to say,
this is not possible for us.*[14]

One might add that, after all, it was possible for the Nazis
to follow the customs of their ancestors. The marshes of the
tribal society had graduated to the death camps of the Nazi
era.

(iv) The Amendment of Paragraph 175 and the
Final Solution of the Gay Problem

Since the earliest days of the Nazis in the 1920s, gays
formed a sizable minority within the movement. Estimates
range between 10% and 13%.[15] Although there are no lists
available indicating the sexual orientation of its members, the
National Socialist Workers Party's emphasis on masculine
vigor, adventure, vitality, and virile camaraderie exercised a
certain attraction on a number of gay people, as well as it did
on non-gay people. Especially the SA-groups around their
flamboyant leader Ernst Roehm, the most prominent gay
person in the Nazi movement, were popular among some
homosexuals because they provided a certain sado-masochis-
tic touch that some gay people might have looked for at the
time.[16] No other social or political group was really interested in the membership of homosexuals. So the rowdy bands
of SA-thugs provided an atmosphere of homeliness and acceptance for many gay Nazis, however strange to be understood.

Nazi gays remained quite naive even after the 1928 Party
statement calling for the extermination of all homosexuals.

They behaved as though they were living in a dream and felt so safe in the bosom of the party that they did not fear anything dangerous could ever happen to them. They were badly mistaken.

In 1934 the SA under its leader Roehm's guidance had become such a powerful force of about 500,000 members, that Hitler perceived them as a threat to his gaining absolute control over all sensitive areas of the Reich. Although he knew about the sexual orientation and gay lifestyle of his old friend Ernst Roehm, Hitler treated it as a matter of personal choice. Hitler was not so much concerned about the homosexual orientation of certain members of the SA. His fear lay rather in their possible attempts as a powerful political group to limit his influence in the political affairs of the Reich. Roehm's homosexuality and that of many SA members served as a welcomed pretext for initiating an all out war against gays throughout the German Reich. Roehm and many of his close associates were arrested on June 30, 1934, in what came to be known as the Blood Purge. They were shot either immediately or on the following day.

A thorough cleaning of the SA of all actual or perceived homosexuals followed. Hitler passed the most stringent edicts against homosexuality which culminated in 1935 in the revision of Paragraph 175 of the German Penal Code. The first order Hitler gave after the Blood Purge to the new chief of the SA was as follows:

> I expect all SA leaders to help preserve and strengthen the SA in its capacity as a pure and clean institution. In particular, I should like every mother to be able to allow her son to join the SA, Party, and Hitler Youth without fear that he may become morally corrupted in their ranks. I therefore require all SA commanders to take the utmost pains to ensure the offenses under Paragraph 175 are met

by immediate expulsion of the culprit from the
SA and the Party.[17]

The amendment to Paragraph 175 was decided upon on June 28, 1935, and became effective September 1, 1935.[18] The extent of the amended paragraph could be felt in 1936, when the number of sentenced homosexual men jumped to between 5,320[19] and 9,081,[20] depending on the source used. This represents a five to tenfold increase over the number of sentences distributed in 1934.

The interpretation of the amended paragraph now listed a whole number of activities as punishable offenses. The acts included such things as a kiss, an embrace, and even homosexual fantasies. As for the latter, in case one wonders how fantasies could be detected, the answer is that many gay—like many non-gay people--write their fantasies down, describe them in letters, or simply talk about them. Another reason for a conviction could be that a voyeur admitted that he had regarded more the man than the woman during a sexual act.[21]

The newly amended paragraph gave the Nazis a handy means to ensnare whomever they wanted to get rid of. Especially the Catholic Church and its institutions were among the victims of the intensified paragraph. Parish houses and monasteries were searched. It was the Nazis' intention to denounce a great part of the clergy and monks as homosexuals. Naturally, they were "successful" in some cases. Of the 21,000 regular priests 57 were accused and convicted; of the 4,000 monks 6; and of the 3,000 lay brethren 170.[22]

The Catholic Church's reaction to the accusations in general was minimal. Because the accusations were in accordance with prevailing law, the Church as an institution kept largely quiet. Rescue activity, if any at all, happened on the level of the individual case out of fear that large scale protest against the Nazi government would result in the rescission of the favors given to the Catholic Church in the 1933 concordate of the Vatican with the German Reich.[23]

From the point of view of sexual morality it seems highly doubtful that the Catholic Church was at all interested in serious protest against the amended verison of the Paragraph. The text of the original Paragraph as well as of sections (a) and (b) of the amended version was very much in accordance with official Catholic moral teaching. A protest, therefore, would have undermined the Church's own position of strong moral condemnation of any kind of homosexual activity, a position that, in principle, has not been changed.

The Nazis were convinced that the new version of the Paragraph also reflected the so called "healthy sensibility" of the people or the "wholesome popular sentiment," which always seems to be one of the worst arguments for anything. They were not entirely wrong in their assumptions. Denunciations of gays and people for whatever reason suspected to be gay were rampant. In fact, people cried "faggot" after whomever they happened to dislike, regardless of the person's actual sexual orientation.

With the effective date of September 1, 1935, of the amended Paragraph 175, the "final solution" of the gay question had begun. It was now in the hands of the regular police force, the Gestapo and the SS guards in the Concentration Camps to apply the new policy.

(v) The Post-war Legal and Social Situation of Gays in the Federal Republic of Germany and the German Democratic Republic

The Penal Code of the German Democratic Republic in 1949 knew a discriminatory paragraph. It seems, however, that judicial practice refrained quite soon from enforcing the law. Reiner Werner interprets this as a rational adjustment of judicial practice to social realities.[24] The Code in its version of January 12, 1968, deleted any specifically anti-gay paragraphs. Instead it lists general paragraphs concerning coercion and sexual abuse, prostitution, sexual activity in public and dissemination of pornographic material (Paragraphs 122 to 125 Penal Code of the GDR).

It is a positive sign that for the first time since 1871 gays were not seen primarily as unequal in the eyes of the law. In that respect the legislation of the GDR has to be commended. A distinction, however, has to be made between legal and social status, legal protection and social acceptance.

The society of the German Democratic Republic has not been indifferent to homosexuality and homosexual activity. Gays were socially just as ostracized in the first "Workers' and Peasants' State" on German soil as they had been in the German Empire, the Weimar Republic and the Third Reich. The social order of the socialist society and its morality also did not have a place for same sex love. The covert suspicion was that homosexuality could in no way contribute to the edification of the socialist state. Again the focus was on procreation. Gays in the GDR could, however, in some way look back to a heritage of early communist support (*e.g.*, in the Weimar Republic). This support was lacking in the bourgeois parties of the West.

Since it has almost been impossible, until very recently, to receive any literature about the past and present situation of gays in the GDR, any interpretation is largely based on speculation.[25] The situation is somewhat different for the Federal Republic of Germany. Legally nothing changed after the war. The Penal Code of the FRG incorporated Paragraph 175 of the German Reich in its Nazi version. This was the situation until the First Criminal Law Reform Act of 1969.

Although a 1968 *Alternative Draft of a Penal Code for the Federal Republic of Germany*[26] called for the complete rescission of the anti-gay paragraph of the criminal law, the legislature did not follow the recommendation. Instead parliament developed a paragraph which saw a punishable offense in homosexual activity with minors, cases of coercion and threat of violence in connection with homosexual activity, homosexual activity with males in a relationship of dependency and homosexual prostitution.

The new Paragraph represented a step into a more liberal direction since it did no longer punish indiscriminately all male homosexual activity. In that respect it was a success for the gay liberation movement in Germany. But it was also far from the recommendations of the Alternative Draft of 1968. Under Title V, that draft dealt with crimes against sexual liberty (Pars. 124-128) and listed specifically rape, sexual intimidation, traffic in human beings, sexual abuse of those incapable of offering resistance, sexual abuse of institutionalized inmates and exhibitionistic conduct. These are all crimes involving violence or coercion. This is exactly absent from homosexual activities among consenting adults, according to the framers of the Alternative Draft. Therefore, those activities should not be subject to provisions of the criminal law.

The current version of the paragraph which was enacted through the Fourth Criminal Law Reform Act of 1973, follows the Alternative Draft recommendations an additional step. Not only homosexual activities engaged in by an adult (*i.e.*, a male over 18 years of age) with a male minor are subject to criminal prosecution. The underlying idea for the renewed reform of the anti-gay paragraph was to guarantee the "undisturbed sexual development of the male adolescent."[27] It is again interesting to note that even the Penal Code of 1973 does not confer independent sexuality on women. There is no law that would make lesbian activity in parallel cases a criminal offense.

Decriminalization of homosexual activity among consenting adult males did not, however, make an end to prejudice and resentment against homosexuality and homosexuals within the society of the FRG. The beginning of the AIDS crisis in Germany had, in fact, quite the opposite effects. The application of a cheap scape-goat theory made it very easy for many Germans, not only among those with limited education and low-level tolerance of social plurality, to vent their hatred again against a societal minority exclusively because of the perception of a threatening difference. The Bavarian AIDS regulations of 1987 that include contact tracing, reporting the names of HIV-positive testees to the state health agency and other rules are the dangerous result of that type of behavior. Even quarantining of PWAs or HIV-positives was seriously discussed among responsible officers in the Bavarian state health department.

Whether it is admitted publicly or not, gays in Germany are still perceived as a threat to the social order. The public majority sees the matrimonial state as the only rightful place for the exercise of sexual activity. Those of a more liberal persuasion who do not want to go that far, at least want to normate heterosexual relationships as the orderly place for sexual activity. Whoever dares to advocate the values of reciprocal love and sharing independently of the type of sexual relationship in which these values are realized is still met with suspicion and evaluated as a social and/or moral anarchist. This happened to representatives of the Greens party in the German parliament. The parliamentary situation might only be a mirror for the dominant sentiment out in the country.

Organized religion in the FRG remains remarkably quiet in the face of all this. As a part of the silent majority it indirectly supports public prejudice and bigotry. Catholic and Protestant churches alike take great pains in dealing with homosexual employees, be they in or out of the closet. If they are in the closet, any problems are dealt with in secrecy. If they have come out of the closet, the churches will quickly and publicly disassociate themselves from these persons, regardless of the good service they might have provided to their employer and their parishioners.

Gay victims of the Nazi terror so far do not get any restitution from the FRG, because the law regards them as criminals who had come into conflict with the standing law

88

of the country. Legal opinion is that they were not persecuted because of race, religion or political conviction.

The government of the FRG stated on October 17, 1979 —and it was a social democratic-liberal coalition government at that time—that

> According to Paragraph 1 of the Federal Restitution Act, a victim of national-socialist persecution is only [he/she] who was persecuted by national-socialist terror measures because of political opposition against national-socialism, or because of reasons of race, religion or faith. This is not applicable to persons taken to Concentration Camps because of homosexuality.[29]

If the German society was willing to break with national-socialism once and for ever, all homosexual Concentration Camp victims should receive reparations. Equally those who were persecuted until 1969 according to the fascist version of the statute. There is an obvious inconsistency in government thinking: The state decriminalized homosexual activity in 1969 and 1973 and yet, in 1979, addresses the situation as if that decriminalization had not taken place. This illustrates the continuing tension between improvement in the laws and stasis in social attitudes.

—Michael L. Stemmeler, Ph.D.

NOTES

[1] Heinz Heger, *Die Maenner mit dem rosa Winkel* (Hamburg, FRG: Merlin Verlag, 1972); English translation: *The Men with the Pink Triangle,* trans. David Fernbach (Boston, MA: Alyson Publications, 1980).

[2] *Op. cit.*, p. 38.

[3] See bibliography at end of Notes.*

[4] Richard Plant, *The Pink Triangle: The Nazi War Against Homosexuals* (New York, NY: Henry Holt and Company, 1986), p. 154. Plant bases his figure on Ruediger Lautmann (ed.), *Seminar: Gesellschaft und Homosexualitaet* (Frankfurt a.M., FRG: Suhrkamp Verlag, 1977), p. 333.

[5] There are no numbers available for January 1945, through May 8, 1945.

[6] One of the sources presents two sets of differing numbers for 1936 to 1939 and lists only the number for the first six months of 1940. A year by year breakdown of sentenced homosexual men can be found in Richard Plant, *The Pink Triangle*, pp. 231-232, and is based on (1) Brigitte Geissler, *Die Homosexuellen-Gesetzgebunt als Instrument der Ausuebung politischer Macht* (Goettingen, FRG: M.A.-thesis, University of Goettingen, 1968), pp. 10, 25; and, (2) Hans-Georg Stuemke and Rudi Finkler, *Rosa Winkel, Rosa Listen: Homosexuelle und "Gesundes Volksempfinden" von Auschwitz bis heute* (Reinbek, FRG: Rowohlt Verlag, 1981), p. 267. In his book *Homosexualitaet: Herausforderung an Wissen und Toleranz* (2d ed., Berlin, GDR: VEB Verlag Volk und Gesundheit, 1988), Reiner Werner, professor of forensic psychology at Humboldt University in Berlin, estimates the number of gays killed by the Nazis to be 150,000 (see p. 17). A figure of 220,000 killed homosexuals is often cited in Gay Liberation articles. Other researchers find it reasonable to conclude that at least 500,000 gays were killed in the Holocaust because of antihomosexual prejudice that consequently led to the Nazi policy of *gaynocide*; see Franz Rector, *The Nazi Extermination of Homosexuals* (Briarcliff Manor, NY: Stein and Day, 1980), p. 116.

[7] See Ruediger Lautmann (ed.), *Seminar: Gesellschaft und Homosexualitaet*, p. 333.

[8] The Wannsee Conference was held in January 1942 in the Wannsee district of Berlin. Its purpose was to decide the fate of European Jewry. The conference developed the idea of the "Final Solution" to the "Jewish Problem." Himmler and Heydrich were ordered to supervise this ultimate persecution of European Jewry, including the transport of Jews to the death camps in eastern Europe.

[9] Thomas Lechie Jarman, *The Rise and Fall of Nazi Germany* (New York, NY: New American Library, 1964).

[10] *Ibid.*, p. 128.

[11] The English text of the paragraph can be found in Eldon R. James (ed.), *The Statutory Criminal Law of Germany. With Comments* (Washington, DC: The Library of Congress, 1947), p. 114.

[12] Joachim Stephan Hohmann (ed.), *Der Unterdrueckte Sexus. Historische Texte und Kommentare zur Homosexualitaet* (Lollar, FRG: Andreas Achenbach Verlag, 1977), p. 241 (translation mine).

[13] James D. Steakley, *The Homosexual Emancipation Movement in Germany* (New York, NY: Arno Press, 1975), p. 84; the German original of the letter was published in Rudolf Klare, *Homosexualitaet und Strafrecht* (Hamburg: Hanseatische Verlagsbuchhandlung, 1937), p. 149.

[14] Bradley Fraser Smith and Agnes F. Peterson (eds.), *Heinrich Himmler: Geheimreden, 1933-1945, und andere Ansprachen* (Frankfurt a.M., FRG: Propylaeen Verlag, 1974) p. 97.

¹⁵Franz Rector arrives at this figure (*op. cit.*, p. 31) by applying the results of Kinsey's statistical study of sexuality in North America to other industrialized nations such as Germany. I would, however, proceed with caution in this judgment.

¹⁶See Franz Rector, *The Nazi Extermination of Homosexuals*, p. 23.

¹⁷Hans Peter Bleul, *Sex and Society in Nazi Germany* (Philadelphia, PA: Lippincott, 1973), pp. 218-219.

¹⁸Text of Paragraph 175, with amendments as issued on June 28, 1935:

175: *A male who commits lustful acts with another male or permits himself to be so abused for lustful acts, shall be punished by imprisonment.*

In the case of a participant under 21 years of age at the time of the commission of the act, the court may, in especially light cases, disregard punishment.

175(a): *Confinement not to exceed ten years and, under extenuating circumstances, imprisonment for not less than three months shall be imposed: (1) Upon a male who, with force or with threat of imminent danger to life and limb, compels another male to conduct lustful acts with him or to compel that other to submit to abuse for lustful acts; (2) Upon a male who, by abuse of a relationship of dependency upon him, in consequence of service, employment or subordination, induces another male to conduct lustful acts with him or to submit himself to abuse for such acts; (3) Upon a male who being over 21 years of age induces another male under 21 years of age to conduct lustful acts with him or to submit himself to abuse for such acts; (4) Upon a male who carries on as a business lustful acts with other men, or submits himself to such abuse by other men, or offers himself for lustful acts with other men.*

175(b): *Unnatural lustful intercourse conducted between human-beings and animals shall be punished by imprisonment, loss of civic rights may also be imposed."* This translation of the amended paragraph can be found in Eldon R. James, *The Statutory Criminal Law of Germany. With Comments*, p. 114.

[19] This is the number according to the official Gestapo statistics for conviction of homosexuals as cited in Brigitte Geissler, *Die Homosexuellen-Gesetzgebung als Instrument der Ausuebung politischer Macht*, p. 10.

[20] Geissler arrives at this number by using an unpublished report of the Federal Security Office for Combating Abortion and Homosexuality for the years 1936-1939, in *ibid.*, p. 25.

[21] See Franz Rector, *The Nazi Extermination of Homosexuals*, p. 119.

[22] Hans Guenter Hockerts, *Die Sittlichkeitsprozesse gegen katholische Ordensangehoerige und Priester, 1936-1937* (Mainz, FRG: Matthias-Gruenwald-Verlag, 1971), pp. 39-41, 48, 50 and 53.

[23] The concordate of 1933 between the Vatican and Nazi Germany still regulates the relationship of state and the Catholic Church in the Federal Republic. It seems that, with the exception of the Greens party, no political party represented in the federal legislature is seriously interested in a reinterpretation of the relationship of church and state. Fear of a reduction of popular support in future elections is most often cited as the reason for this reluctance.

[24] Reiner Werner, *Homosexualitaet: Herausforderung an Wissen und Toleranz*, p. 17.

25 The *Second ILGA Pink Book. A Global View of Lesbian and Gay Liberation and Oppression* edited by the Pink Book Editing Team (Utrecht Series on Gay and Lesbian Studies. nr. 12; Utrecht, NL: Interfacultaire Werkgroep Homostudies, Rijksuniversiteit Utrecht, 1988) includes an article on lesbian women in the German Democratic Republic by Ilse Kokula ("The Situation and Organization of Lesbian Women in the German Democratic Republic," pp. 133-142) who has worked for a number of years in the GDR. The book also mentions a 1985 congress on "Psychosocial Aspects of Homosexuality," which took place in Leipzig.

26 Juergen Baumann (ed.), *Alternative Draft of a Penal Code for the Federal Republic of Germany*, trans. and with an introduction by Joseph J. Darby (The American Series of Foreign Penal Codes, no. 21; South Hackensack, NJ: Fred Rotman and Co. ; London, GB: Sweet and Maxwell Limited, 1977).

27 See the commentary to Paragraph 175 in its 1973 version in Eduard Dreher (ed.), *Strafgesetzbuch mit Nebengesetzen und Verordnungen* (Munich, FRG: C. H. Beck'sche Verlagsbuchhandlung, 36th, revised edition, 1976), p. 686.

28 Hans-Georg Stuemke and Rudi Finkler, *Rosa Winkel, Rosa Listen: Homosexuelle und "Gesundes Volksempfinden" von Auschwitz bis heute* (Reinbeck, FRG: Rowohlt Verlag, 1981), p. 418.

---

* The bibliography has been omitted in interest of space by the editors.

Associated Press

Richard Butler, left, head of the Aryan Nations white suprema-cist group and pastor of the Church of Jesus Christ Christian-Aryan Nations, is flanked by supporters at a march

Theological and Ethical Implications of
Homophobic Violence

In moving to a consideration of the theological and ethical implications of homophobic violence, I shall organize my
discussion under the following subtopics: (i) empirical data,
(ii) adolescence, (iii) gender-role socialization, (iv) the Book
of Leviticus from Hebrew scripture, and (v) a conclusion.

(i) Data

In 1987 I conducted a national survey of lesbians and gay
men to ascertain the rate and characteristics of physical violence directed at them by non-lesbian/gay people because of
their sexual orientation. I found that fifty-three percent of
the respondents had been victims of anti-gay/lesbian violence.
This percentage was the same as that found in two other sur-
veys: one of lesbians and gay men in the State of Maine, and
the other of lesbians and gay men in the City of Philadelphia.[1] Incidents range from being chased to being beaten,
bludgeoned, and stabbed.

Victims in my survey report that ninety-four percent of
the perpetrators are male. Nearly one-half are twenty-one
years of age and younger; the great majority (eighty percent)
are less than twenty-eight years old.

When compared with perpetrators of violent crime in general, perpetrators of anti-gay/lesbian violence tend to be
younger, are more often male, and more frequently outnum-
ber their victims.[2]

Interviews with teenage perpetrators show that attacking
gay men and lesbians is not an expression of hatred and disapproval as much as it is a recreational option. Of course,
expressions of hatred and disapproval are foremost in many
incidents; but perpetrators most frequently say that their
attacks are a source of adventure and enjoyment.[3] Law en-

forcement and community agency personnel familiar with teenage perpetrators point out that assailants consider these attacks "a kind of sport" that is a custom and tradition. One agency director reports: "In some communities, it is seen as a rite of passage among males, sanctioned, if not admired, by the community elders."[4]

Data taken from courtroom trials in which victims have been killed reveal a paucity of criminal records and psychological disorders among perpetrators. Psychiatric and law enforcement professionals observe that assailants do not typically exhibit what are customarily thought of as criminal attitudes and behaviors. Many are models of middle-class respectability.[5]

Perpetrators represent the range of socio-economic classes and appear to be, for the most part, quite ordinary or average young men within all classes and racial groups. The predominant characteristics are age and gender. The typical perpetrator is an adolescent male who acts in the company of other adolescent males.

(ii) Adolescence

Professor of human development and education Mihaly Czikzsentmihalyi reminds us that the conception of "adolescence" itself is recent. Less than a century ago, at puberty teenagers customarily took on the role of "full-fledged human beings" as wives, husbands, parents, workers. Adolescence has subsequently become inserted between childhood and adulthood as "a kind of temporal warehouse or greenhouse in which young people are parked until needed." "In terms of physical and mental vitality, teenagers are at the top of the arch of life," but feel "that they have been put on hold ... while their best years drift by." For teenagers, "waiting for [social] maturity is often frustrating." A measure of this frustration is found in data collected by Czikzsentmihalyi which show that teenagers "report being significantly less strong, active, alert, and, especially, less motivated" than adults, including senior citizens. He concludes "that teenagers feel their position to be one of weakness and constraint" because they are not encouraged or allowed to use whatever skills or aptitudes they have to interact effectively with their environment. Scholars in the field of adolescent development agree that if adults do not treat young people "as fully formed persons who should be responsible for their lives, and who should have access to meaningful experiences" we should not be suprised that they will "learn to enjoy activities that cause harm to others" and themselves.[6]

Concluding, however, that anti-gay/lesbian violence is simply compensation for the frustration, boredom, alienation and inferiority associated with the social position of teenagers is not sufficient. It would follow, also, that those adolescents who are poorest, most underprivileged and nonachieving would be the most likely assailants, which the data on anti-gay/lesbian violence does not show. Teenage women, who seem to have even less status and power than teenage men, are conspicuously under-represented among perpetrators (even more so than in statistics for criminal violence in general). Perpetrators are not only predominantly male, but just as, or even more likely, to be: from middle-class families; getting good grades; involved in school and community activities, organizations, and athletics; popular, friendly, and sociable; taking college-preparatory courses in high school or enrolled in college, and in the military.

While the socially-constructed powerlessness of adolescence is causally-related to the perpetration of anti-gay/lesbian violence, it is a partial cause. A full explanation must consider the socialization of men.

(iii) Gender-role socialization

Studies of gender-roll socialization show that males in our society are expected and taught to be socially and physically aggressive and sexually dominant, while warmth, emotional expressiveness, and being sensitive, supporting, nurturing, noncompetitive, and not dominant are considered positive traits for women. Not only are young men expected and encouraged to develop skills in dominance and violence, they more than young women conform to gender-role expectations and are more likely to victimize those who do not.[7]

That young men would be the most frequent perpetrators of anti-gay/lesbian violence would seem to follow from these data. Young men are expected to accept the inferiority attached to their age and the superior status assigned to their gender. To off-set their lack of real control and participation in the social order, adolescent males do not have recourse (either through marriage or gainful employment) to the privilege or power accorded adult men.

One consequence or resolution of the contradictory message to be powerful while not having any real power is violence directed by adolescent males against children, women their own age, members of marginalized ethnic and racial groups, and lesbians and gay men. In an informal survey of college freshmen, I have found that sixteen percent of the male respondents report having physically attacked lesbians and gay men. This rate is similar to that for sexual assault of women and children by adolescent males. Studies and reports on bias-related violence indicate that lesbians and gay men are victimized at a rate greater than individuals in ethnic and racial groups.[8]

Adolescence, therefore, as a socially-constructed stage of human development in which skills-training, challenges, and opportunities do not meet the real potential, interests, and needs of teenagers, fosters power-seeking, adventurist recreational activities at the expense of others who, also, do not have power within the social order. Engaging in these activities, for the most part, are those who have been socialized to be physically aggressive and to resolve problems with violence. The simultaneity of this socialization and the denial of their having real social power and status is dangerous for lesbians and gay men.

(iv) Bible

The Book of Leviticus is explicit in condemning male homosexuality and prescribing capital punishment for those practicing it.[9] It, also, mandates love for one's neighbor and for the stranger who sojourns with you. For our times, prescribing both death for gay men as well as love for the stranger would seem to be contradictory. How can one both love and kill those who are other, marginal, outsiders, strangers?

An initial exegesis of Leviticus shows that its "love of neighbor and stranger" is not the same as what some of us may interpret to mean love of those who are outside of the familiar social circle. The Hebrew term for sojourner or stranger (*ger*) has little if anything to do with outcasts or marginal people.[10] It is more accurately translated as "resident alien," one who was born elsewhere but lives and works as an accepted member and according to the standards of the community. The term for neighbor (*rea'*), immediately adjacent to and interchangeable with terms for companion (*'amit*), brother (*'ah*), and fellow countryman (*ben-'am*), reinforces homogeneity as the condition for communal love.[11] To love neighbor and sojourner is to love those who are immediate to and most like oneself.

One looks in vain for an example of inclusive community, egalitarian principles, or a theology of loving outreach and pluralistic justice in Leviticus. Leviticus is about defining a separate community, setting itself apart by virtue of its superior difference with others.[12] Its cultic regulations delineate precisely who may be inside and who will be put outside, in its own terms, "cut from their people."[13] Its social legislation mandates mutual support among those who are inside.[14] Concern for the poor, widows and orphans, a theme recurring throughout Judaeo-Christian scripture, is conspicuously absent here, replaced by concern for oneself and those within one's familial organization.[15]

Leviticus should be understood in terms of the times in which and the reasons for which it was compiled and written.[16] Two events shaped this document: (1) the Fall of Jerusalem in 586 BCE with its subsequent dispersion or exile; and, (2) the decree by Cyrus, the Persian emperor, forty-nine years later to restore Israel as an autonomous religious community.

Biblical scholars and historians tell us that the dispersion (or exile) was "a forced removal of royalty, state officials, priests, army officers, and artisans who probably constituted no more than 5 percent of the total populace."[17] The edict of Cyrus allowed them to return. This was part of a wider policy of extending to certain subject people considerable autonomy and respect for their indigenous cultural and religious life when such was an advantage to the Persian empire. It was to Persia's advantage to prevent a weak point of defense in the west by stabilizing Jerusalem. To avoid granting it political independence, Persia encouraged and backed the development of Jerusalem's religious autonomy and the codifying of the religious laws as the basis for colonial law.[18]

For returning Babylonian exiles, "a 'declassed' elite who had formerly known excessive privilege" as the upperclass of Jerusalem, the choices were limited but obvious. With political independence and the restoration of the monarchy as the remotest of possibilities, these exiles returned committed to reviving, reforming, and restoring Israel's religious tradition, custom, cult, and history. Restoring Israel as an autonomous religious community "was a political act initiated and imposed upon the Jewish community by the collaboration of Persian imperial authorities and a Jewish colonial elite imported from the exile to Judah."[19]

The Book of Leviticus attempts to re-interpret the

history of Israel in favor of these new developments. The post-exilic formalization of cultic practices, social regulations, and the organization of priests are set and legitimated in the context of Yahweh's speaking to Moses at Sinai. Routine practices which are mentioned in the Book of Exodus become elaborated and elevated in the Book of Leviticus to resolve Jerusalem's current socioeconomic problems in favor of the returning exiles. For example, the observance of Sabbath is not merely a provision for regularly scheduled rest but becomes institutionalized as "the Jubilee year," a means to return land and property to those who had left them. The attempt by the returning, former ruling class to establish an historical precedent for the consolidation and control of Israel's religious community is transparent.[20]

(v) Conclusion

The contradiction initially apparent in Leviticus' dual prescriptions of love for the stranger and death for homosexuals is illusory. It does not foster a debate that might produce a corrective norm for the problem of anti-gay/lesbian violence. However, the overarching concern in this document —which is the establishment of a separate, exclusive community—does offer insight into the problem of such violence in our times because the motive and cause are similar to both.

The parallels are apparent. For example:

(1) An adolescent male in North America today is likely to demonstrate aggressive, dominant, violent behavior against those who are socially even less powerful because it is one of the few options open to him, especially if he wants to conform to appropriate gender-role behavior and maintain the gender-role privilege expected of and by men.

(2) By comparison, a Babylonian exile returned to Jerusalem to establish a ruling religious elite because it was

one of the few options open to him, especially if he wanted to demonstrate a measure of upperclass behavior and maintain the status expected of and by the upperclass.

This favoring of a particular group—adolescent males or declassed exiles—was and is by design of and benefit to those who control the social order. To continue the parallel:

(1) Those least likely to accept the boredom and lack of challenge in adolescence are males because they are also socialized to be aggressive, adventuresome, and in control. Permission for "boys to be boys" (*i.e.*, to victimize sissies, queers, deviants) suffices to hold them in check with "minor league" male status but also reinforces social standards. The high rates of and benign regard for date rape[21] and homophobic violence among teenagers indicate the willingness with which male dominance and standards of deviance are enforced.

(2) By comparison, those most likely to be restless and least likely to accept continued exile and powerlessness after Cyrus's decree are those who had been socialized as the ruling elite of Jerusalem. By permitting their return to establish a religiously autonomous, but politically dependent, community, Persia was able to use their eagerness to stabilize a weak spot on the western border of the Empire. This, too, like that of our adolescent males, was "minor league" autonomy in service of the greater Persian social order.

An important question for my work is: Does the establishing of special, but limited, privilege and power for a group within a social order mean that lesbians and gay men will be the likely or inevitable targets for physical attack, punishment, or exclusion by that group? And I would say yes, if the social order which is maintained by and grants the group its limited privilege is patriarchal. The condition on which young men are permitted to behave as they do is the conformity of their behavior to standards of heterosexual male control and superiority. By comparison, on the condition that they supported and conformed to the imperial order, the exiles were allowed to return. The hierarchical priestly organization of "unblemished," married heterosexual males that they established to rule their separate community reflected the organizing principles of the social order to which they owed allegiance;[22] their prescribing capital punishment for gay men underscored the eagerness with which they would enforce those principles.

We can be sure that if the practice of teenage males were the targeting of corporate executives or married men, the social response to their activities would be markedly different than it is to their targeting lesbians and gay men. And we can be sure that the returning exiles would not have gotten far if their intention in returning to Israel had been to promote a gynocentric, egalitarian, open mode of worship and familial organization. In exchange for a measure of control and power, each group enthusiastically distinguishes itself from, punishes, or victimizes those whose freedom would violate the organizing principle of the social order which grants the group its limited but special privileges.

What are the ethical and theological implications of anti-gay/lesbian violence in terms of an understanding that can be gained from a reading of Leviticus?

I use the term "ethical" to mean doing that which we need to do to become fully human.[23] And here the ethical implication goes beyond the immediate arena of male adolescent behavior:

The lesbian/gay movement has come of age during a post-World War II period of the U.S.'s economic growth and international power. Without intending to undermine either the gains lesbians and gay men have made or the suffering we have endured, I would suggest that we have been tolerated and become more visible in a country which has enjoyed stability and expansion for forty years. Its thrust has not been to exclude and define itself narrowly because its position has not been threatened or uncertain. However, if predictions about its future loss of stature and economic stability are accurate, we can expect that, if this proud nation loses the power and privilege to which it is accustomed, it will seek new ways in which to exercise its authority, however reduced and limited. An early signal of efforts to prove itself powerful in the face of its diminishing standing may be the invasion of Grenada and the bombast with which it was justified as a successful rescue operation.[24]

Few, I'm sure, are not aware of the U.S.'s federal deficit and the change in fiscal policy introduced by the Reagan administration. The 1980s broke with a remarkably long history of a steady debt-income ratio; the more-than-doubling of federal indebtedness in this decade, with the size of the nation's economy increasing by barely half, is unprecedented. Until 1981 the U.S. had been a creditor nation and increasingly so; the new fiscal policy has transformed it from a creditor to a debtor nation. World power and influence have historically accrued to creditor countries; Japan and West Germany have now emerged as the world's largest creditors. The U.S. is not in a position to simply regain lost power. Assets and position have already been transferred, or the momentum of the process is so great as to be irreversible. Foreign investors will not likely give them or sell them back to the U.S. simply out of kindness. And the changes will include not only a reduction in the U.S.'s international influence and the increase in foreign control of business here, but a greatly reduced standard of living for individuals.[25]

Domestic solutions will be neither easily implemented nor adjusted to without great alarm and hardship by American workers and consumers. In the past, such efforts to remedy much smaller deficits have created recessions; and those will seem minuscule compared to one caused by trying to narrow today's enormous deficit. Also, typically in recessions, difficulties do not fall equally on all people. Inequalities would multiply enormously. When the reduction of American incomes required to restore international equilibrium does occur, the effect will be harsher than ever before. When standards of living plummet, especially among groups, conflicts and boundaries between groups will most likely sharpen.[26]

You have probably noticed signs of the deterioration of the liberal social agenda of the sixties and seventies. The defeat of the Equal Rights Amendment;[27] the defeat of or difficulties in passing proposed gay/lesbian rights legislation and the repeal of some that had been passed;[28] the resurgence of arguments for and the implementation of "a return to classical pedagogy;"[29] the documented widening gap between rich and poor;[30] the Supreme Court's *Bowers v. Hardwick* decision, its decision to allow censorship of high school student newspapers, its unsolicited request to hear argument concerning one of the most fundamental places of civil rights legislation, and its reconsidering and possibly overturning *Roe v. Wade.*[31] Increases in reports of sexist, anti-semitic, racist, and anti-gay/lesbian incidents on college campuses and in the public sphere[32] may be reactions that support these policy statements, reflect in individual behavior the loss of or desperate attempt to regain power nationally, and/or express a perceived loss of social and economic status by those individuals who feel entitled to it. The tendency toward the precise formulation of restrictions in matters of daily life and sexuality does not seem unlike that observed in Leviticus. The exaggerated and desperate grasp for power in the face of diminishing national standing may tie us to the situation in Leviticus and let us use that document for understanding what we can do during our times.

If we have begun to expect and rely on a progressive social agenda which assumes eventual equality, our reading of Leviticus should show us that some abrupt turnabouts could easily disrupt and threaten our expectations and practice.

As a nation whose social order remains patriarchal, its desperate attempts to recount and redefine its authority along traditional lines would mean a renewed emphasis on heterosexual male superiority; and lesbian and gay men would be identified and targeted more emphatically and by more than male adolescents. If we have begun to expect and rely on the progressing liberation of lesbian and gay men as demonstrated during the past forty years, the ethical implication of a study of anti-gay/lesbian violence from a biblical perspective is that we should seriously consider and prepare for a change of events.

The theological implication continues this line of thinking. I use the term "theological" to mean that which is personal, relational, and transformative.[33]

I am reminded of the remarks by a gay man at a memorial service five years ago in New York City for those who had died of AIDS and homophobic violence. He had lived in Berlin before Hitler's rise and had managed to escape. He was direct in saying that he wanted to convey a particular message very clearly. He told us that if anyone had tried to tell him and his friends what was going to happen in Germany, none of them would have believed it. He said that to be a gay man in Berlin was to feel so free that he could not imagine that it would ever end. The experience of that day, especially as I have studied anti-gay/lesbian violence and attempted to work as a gay scholar and live as a gay person, remains normative for me today and continues to change me. I work (1) with the understanding that there is no safe place for a gay man; and, (2) with the purpose of making a place in which we are taken seriously. We cannot assume that things will get better for us. We have seen rights legislation passed after prolonged effort only to be repealed with great speed; we have heard the highest court decide against us even when it meant violating its own precedent of protecting privacy. I would say that gay scholars need to develop skills and tools that will allow us to anticipate and to prepare for what may happen. While much biblical scholarship has attempted to minimize the homophobia and anti-gay violence of Leviticus, I have tried to read it for what it might tell us about the problems we may face.

—Gary David Comstock, Ph.D.

NOTES

[1] Maine Civil Liberties Union, Maine Lesbian/Gay Political Alliance, and University of Southern Maine Department of Social Welfare, "Discrimination and Violence Survey of Gay People in Maine," (Portland, Maine: University of Southern Maine Department of Social Welfare, 1985); and Steven K. Aurand, Rita Addessa, and Christine Bush, *Violence and Discrimination Against Philadelphia Lesbian and Gay People: A Study by the Philadelphia Lesbian and Gay Task Force* (Philadelphia: Philadelphia Lesbian and Gay Task Force, 1985).

[2] Source used for comparison: Bureau of Justice Statistics, *Criminal Victimization in the United States, 1984: A National Crime Survey Report* NCJ-100435 (Washington, D.C.: U.S. Department of Justice, May 1986).

[3] See Eric Weissman, "Kids Who Attack Gays," *Christopher Street* (August 1978), pp. 9-13.

[4] Lee Ellenberg, "Counseling Service for Gay and Lesbian Victims," (Boston: Mental Health Department of Fenway Community Health Center, 5 February 1986), p. 2 (photocopied).

[5] See: Philip Plews, "The Evil that Boys Do," *Toronto*

108

(May 1986), p. 63; and, Peter Canellos, "A City and Its Sins: The Killing of a Gay Man in Bangor," *Boston Phoenix* (13 November 1984).

[6] Mihaly Csikszentmihalyi, "The Pressured World of Adolescence," *Planned Parenthood Review* (Spring 1986), p. 3. See, also: Mihaly Csikszentmihalyi and Reed Larson, *Being Adolescent. Conflict and Growth in the Teenage Years* (New York: Basic Books, Inc., Publishers, 1984), p. 244.

[7] See: Dorothy I. Riddle and Barbara Sang, "Psychotherapy with Lesbians," *Journal of Social Issues* 34 (1978): 85; Norma Costrich, Joan Feinstein, Louise Kidder, Jeanne Marecek, and Linda Pascale, "When Stereotypes Hurt: Three Studies in Penalties for Sex Role Reversals," *Journal of Experimental Social Psychology* 11 (1975): 520-532; Inge K. Broverman, Susan Raymond Vogel, Donald M. Broverman, Frank E. Clarkson, and Paul S. Rosenkrantz, "Sex Role Stereotypes: A Current Appraisal," *Journal of Social Issues* 28 (1972): 57-58; Rae Carlson, "Stability and Change in Adolescents' Self-Image," *Child Development* 36 (1965): 659-666; Beverly I. Fagot and Isabelle Littman, "Stability of Sex Role and Play Interests from Preschool to Elementary School," *Journal of Psychology* 89 (1975): 285-292; Charles Berger, "Sex Differences Related to Self-Esteem Factor Structure," *Journal of Consulting and Clinical Psychology* 32 (1968): 442-446; David M. Connell and James E. Johnson, "Relationship Between Sex-Role Identification and Self-Esteem in Early Adolescents," *Developmental Psychology* 3 (1970): 268; and, John Hollander, "Sex Differences in Sources of Social Self-Esteem," *Journal of Consulting and Clinical Psychology* 38 (1972): 343-347.

[8] See: Judith V. Becker, Jerry Cunningham-Rathner, and Meg S. Kaplan, "Adolescent Sexual Offenders: Demographics, Criminal and Sexual Histories, and Recommendations for

Reducing Future Offenses," *Journal of Interpersonal Violence* 1 (December 1986): 431-445; Marie Fortune, *Sexual Violence: The Unmentionable Sin* (New York: Pilgrim Press, 1983), pp. 181-183; M. Joan McDermott, *Rape Victimization in 26 American Cities: Applications of the National Crime Survey Victimization and Attitude Data*, Analytic Report SD-VAD-6, Bureau of Justice Statistics (Washington, D.C.: Department of Justice, 1979), p. 12; Peter Finn and Taylor McNeil, *The Response of the Criminal Justice System to Bias Crime: An Exploratory Review*, submitted to National Institute of Justice, U.S. Department of Justice, Contract No. OJP-86-002 (Cambridge, MA: Abt Associates, Inc., 7 October 1987), pp. 1-2; and, Douglas H. White (chair), *Governor's Task Force on Bias-Related Violence, Final Report* (Albany, NY: New York State Government [Mario M. Cuomo, Governor] March 1988), p. 97.

[9] Leviticus 18:22 and 20:13. See: Martin Noth, *Leviticus: A Commentary*, trans. J. E. Anderson, (Old Testament Library; Philadelphia: Westminster Press, 1965), pp. 146-151.

[10] See: Noth, *Leviticus*, pp. 131, 144; Roland de Vaux, *Ancient Israel*, vol. 1: *Social Institutions* (New York: McGraw-Hill Book Co., Inc., 1961; reprinted 1965), p. 74; Norman K. Gottwald, *The Tribes of Yahweh: A Sociology of the Religion of Liberated Israel, 1250-1050 B.C.E.* (Maryknoll, NY: Orbis Books, 1979), p. 291; Mayer Sulzberger, *The Status of Labor in Ancient Israel* (Philadelphia: Dropsie College for Hebrew and Cognate Learning, 1923), pp. 16, 21-22, 25-26, 49, 51, 63-65, 86, 117-121; John Peter Lange, "Exodus, or, The Second Book of Moses," trans. Charles M. Mead, *A Commentary on the Holy Scriptures*, vol. 2 (New York: Scribner, Armstrong and Co., 1876), p. 145; and, S. R. Driver, "The Book of Leviticus," in *The Sacred Books of the Old and New Testaments* (New York: Dodd, Mead and Co., 1898), p. 87. For references, see Leviticus 16:29; 17:8, 10,

12, 13, 15; 18:26; 19:10, 33, 34; 20:2; 22:18; 23;22; 24:16, 22; 25:6, 23, 45, 47.

[11]See: Noth, *Leviticus*, pp. 48-50, 141-142; and Gordon J. Wenham, *The Book of Leviticus* (New International Commentary on the Old Testament; Grand Rapids, MI: William B. Eerdmans Publishing Co., 1979), pp. 266-267.

[12]See, for example, Leviticus 20:22-26.

[13]See: Noth, *Leviticus*, pp. 16-17, 84-85, 91-92, 105-110, 121-125, 151, 160; Wenham, *The Book of Leviticus*, pp. 281-286; Nathaniel Micklem, "The Book of Leviticus," *The Interpreter's Bible* Vol. 2 (New York. Abingdon-Cokesbury Press, 1953), pp. 25, 27-38, 88; Norman K. Gottwald, *The Hebrew Bible—A Socio-Literary Introduction* (Philadelphia: Fortress Press, 1985), p. 476; Mary Douglas, *Purity and Danger: An Analysis of Concepts of Pollution and Taboo* (London: Routledge and Kegan Paul, 1966; reprint 1979), p. 51; and, Robert North, *Sociology of the Biblical Jubilee*, Analecta Biblica Investigationes Scientificae in Res Biblicas 4 (Rome: Pontifical Biblical Institute, 1954), pp. 222-223, 330.

For references to "cutting off," see Leviticus 7:20, 21, 25, 27; 16:15-22; 17:4; 18:24-30; 20:5, 17, 18. To review the theme of "inside/outside" see Leviticus 4:11-12; 6:11; 10:4-5; 13:46; 14:40-45; 16:20-22; 17:3-4; 18:24-30; 21:12; 24:13-23.

[14]See: Noth, *Leviticus*, pp. 185-187, 191-193; Micklem, "The Book of Leviticus," pp. 124-125; de Vaux, *Social Institutions*, p. 75; North, *Sociology of the Biblical Jubilee*, pp. 143-144, 158; George F. Genung, "The Book of Leviticus," *An American Commentary on the Old Testament* ([Nashville, TN:] American Baptist Publication Society, 1905), p. 80; James L. Mays, *Leviticus, Numbers* (Layman's Bible Com-

mentaries; London: SCM Press, Ltd., 1963), p. 59; and, A. R. S. Kennedy, *Leviticus and Numbers* (Century Bible; Edinburgh: T.C.E. and E.C. Jack [1938]), pp. 169-170.

[15]See: Noth, *Leviticus*, pp. 185-187, 191-192; H. Eberhard von Waldow, "Social Responsibility and Social Structure in Early Israel," *Catholic Biblical Quarterly* 32 (1970): 182; and, North, *Sociology of the Bible Jubilee*, pp. 143-144, 215-216.
Provisions for feeding the poor (*ani*) are mentioned in Leviticus 19:10 and 23:22; but widows and orphans are not mentioned. Allowances for those "who cannot afford to participate in cultic practices are prescribed in Leviticus 5:7-13; 12.8; 14.21-32; and 27:8.

[16]See: Noth, *Leviticus*, pp. 10-15; Driver, "The Book of Leviticus," p. 57; Micklem, "The Book of Leviticus," pp. 3-4; Mays, *Leviticus, Numbers*, p. 55; Kennedy, *Leviticus and Numbers*, pp. 15-16; de Vaux, *Social Institutions*, p. 48, and Vol. 2, *Religious Institutions*, p. 482; and Martin Noth, *A History of Pentateuchal Traditions*, trans. Bernhard W. Anderson (Englewood Cliffs, NJ: Prentice-Hall, 1972), pp. 8-9.

[17]Gottwald, *The Hebrew Bible*, p. 423. See, also: Martin Noth, *The History of Israel* (New York: Harper & Row, 1958 [2d ed. 1960]) ., pp. 272-296.

[18]See: Gottwald, *The Hebrew Bible*, pp. 424-425, 428-429, 432; and Noth, *The History of Israel*, p. 318.

[19]Gottwald, *The Hebrew Bible*, p. 437, 460-462, 491. See, also. Noth, *The History of Israel*, pp. 314-315, 317-318, 322-323, 330, 333, 338-339.

[20]See: Noth, *The History of Israel*, pp. 297, 330, 314-316, Noth, *Leviticus*, pp. 129-130, 140, 165-166, 176-177,

183-189, 200-201; Gottwald, *The Hebrew Bible*, pp. 424-425, 460-463; and North, *Sociology of the Biblical Jubilee*, pp. 45, 143-144, 158, 175, 222-223.

[21] See: Laurel Fingley, "Teenagers in Survey Condone Forced Sex," *Ms.* (February 1981), p. 23.

[22] See: Noth, *Leviticus*, pp. 56-57, 153-163. For references, see: Leviticus 6:18, 29; 7:6; 21:1ff; 22:1ff. For a discussion on the devaluation of women, see: Noth, *Leviticus*, pp. 97, 204-205; and, Kennedy, *Leviticus and Numbers*, pp. 177-178. For references, see: Leviticus 12:2-5; 27:1-8.

[23] My formulation here is derived from my reading and understanding of: Paulo Freire, *The Pedagogy of the Oppressed*, trans. Myra Bergman Ramos (1970: New York: Continuum Publishing Corp., 1985); and Audre Lorde, *Sister Outsider: Essays and Speeches* (Trumansburg, NY: Crossing Press, 1984).

[24] For social commentary, see, for example, Lorde, *Sister Outsider*, pp. 176-190.

[25] See, for example, Benjamin Friedman, *Day of Reckoning: the Consequences of American Economic Policy Under Reagan and After* (New York: Random House, 1988).

[26] See: Friedman, *Day of Reckoning.*

[27] See: Beverly Wildung Harrison, "The Equal Rights Amendment: A Moral Analysis," in *Making the Connections: Essays in Feminist Social Ethics*, ed. Carol S. Robb (Boston: Beacon Press, 1985), pp. 167-173.

[28] Arthur S. Leonard, "Gay & Lesbian Rights Protection in the U.S.: An Introduction to Gay and Lesbian Civil

Rights," (Washington, D.C.: National Gay and Lesbian Task Force [1989]).

[29]See: Rick Simonson and Scott Walker (eds.), "Introduction," *The Graywolf Annual Five: Multi-Cultural Literacy* (St. Paul, MN: Graywolf Press, 1988), pp. ix-xv.

[30]See: Hyman Bookbinder, "Did the War on Poverty Fail?" *New York Times* (20 August 1980), sec. 4, p. 23; and, Leonard Silk, "Now, To Figure Why the Poor Get Poorer," *New York Times* (18 December 1988), sec. 4, pp. 1, 5.

[31]See. Linda Greenhouse, "The Court's Shift to the Right," *New York Times* (7 June 1989), sec. A, pp. 1, 22.

[32]See: Lee A. Daniels, "Prejudice on Campuses Is Feared to Be Rising," *New York Times* (31 October 1988), sec. A, p. 12; "Wide Harassment of Women Working for U.S. Is Reported," *New York Times* (1 July 1988), sec. B, p. 6; Peter Applebome, "Two Sides of the Contemporary South: Racial Incidents and Black Progress," *New York Times* (21 November 1989), sec. A, p. 22; and, William R. Greer, "Violence Against Homosexuals Rising, Groups Seeking Wider Protection Say," *New York Times* (23 November 1986), sec. A, p. 36.

[33]My formulation here is derived from my reading and understanding of: Toni Morrison, *Sula* (New York: Alfred A. Knopf, 1973; New American Library, Plume Book, 1982); Carter Heyward, *The Redemption of God: A Theology of Mutual Relation* (Washington, D.C.: University Press of America, 1982); Erich Fromm, *You Shall Be As Gods: A Radical Interpretation of the Old Testament and Its Tradition* (New York: Fawcett Premier, 1969; Ballantine Books, 1983), Beth Brant (Degonwadonti), *Mohawk Trail* (Ithaca, NY: Firebrand Books, 1985); and, Hermann Hesse, *Sidd-*

hartha, trans. Hilda Rosner (New York: New Directions, 1951).

THE
CONTEMPORARY
SITUATION

"A critique of the contemporary situation of homophobia in (organized) religion and society, the first article in this section investigates word and meaning in ecclesiastical statements on human sexuality, sexual orientation, and genital activity. Next is a focus on the Janus-faced quality of the AIDS crisis. On the one hand, it can be utilized to legitimate homophobia and to assist in the generation of socially disruptive legislation which receives the blessing of the leaders of organized religion; on the other hand, the crisis can serve to amalgamate a grassroots militancy for change in religion and society. In that respect the AIDS crisis could be interpreted as a catalyst for change. The last paper in this section explores the interconnection of homophobia and AIDS from the psychoanalytic perspective. The elliptical poles of fear and passion serve as the backdrop against which rationalizations of homophobia, as well as the dynamics of homosexual attraction and revulsion, are projected."

Pope Paul VI (1963–1978) at the altar of Saint Peter's in Rome presides over a session of the Second Vatican Council. The gathering initiated more changes in the Roman Catholic Church than had any development since the Council of Trent in the sixteenth century. [Archivio Fotografico, Musei Vatacani.]

The Evolution of Pastoral Thought
Concerning Homosexuality in
Selected Vatican and American Documents
from 1975-1986

The document *Persona humana*, the *Declaration on Certain Questions Concerning Sexual Ethics*, was issued by the Vatican's Sacred Congregation for the Doctrine of the Faith (CDF) in 1975. It was a response to the Second Vatican Council's recognition that society and the Church should value and utilize the social sciences in a positive, informative manner (*Gaudium et Spes*, 54, 57). *Persona humana* was a bi-product of this recommendation, for the influence of the social sciences is evident in the methodology used in writing the document.

Eleven years later, the Vatican's 1986 *Letter to the World's Bishops on the Pastoral Care of Homosexual Persons*, issued by the CDF shows a different inclination. It does not demonstrate a similarly-informed methodology. Between these two documents a number of pastoral documents from the United States were issued. For the most part these writings restated the Vatican's official position. However a few documents did emerge which pushed the limits of the Church's position on homosexuality up to and beyond the 1975 document's parameters.[1]

(i) Some Preliminary Observations on Language
and Terminology

The most important aspect of the language and terminology being used in the majority of the works cited within is a major assumption concerning the quality of *homosexual acts*. Such actions are commonly and regularly categorized as **intrinsice malum**, that is, **intrinsically evil** acts. These are actions which no Christian ought to ever perform under any circumstance. The Church traditionally had detected such intrinsic evil in only three areas: (1) violations of the marriage contract; (2) the direct taking of an innocent life; and (3) in sexual behavior within "the free exercise of the sexual faculty apart from normal sexual intercourse within a marriage relationship, no matter what the intention or the situation."[2]

Actions of this latter category are seen to significantly fail to reach the full potential of human goodness and possibility, and are evil regardlss of whatever concrete situation in which they occur. Therefore acts termed as **intrinscially evil** would be so because of a high degree of inherent defectiveness as well as being *self-evidently* evil.[3] Among actions which would fall into this category would be all homosexual activity. The difficulty with the categorization of certain sexual actions or activities as intrinsically evil is that

> *norms should exist . . . but that [such actions]*
> *should be viewed as involving absolute and ex-*
> *ceptionless standards different . . . [creates] a*
> *legalism which does injustice to both the Crea-*
> *tor and his creation.*[4]

However, despite theologians' arguments, the standard is retained for usage in the pronouncements made by Church authorities. The terminology used is static and non-experiental in its perspective. In its most traditionalist statement, homosexuality emerges, in the words of Karl Barth, as

> *the physical, pathological and social sickness,*
> *the phenomenon of perversion, decadence and*
> *decay, which can emerge when man refuses to*
> *admit the validity of the divine command.*[5]

Person and action were considered a unity: not only was the homosexual action considered impermissible and intrinsically evil, but the homosexual person also was subject to similar opprobrium. This restricted view of homosexuality was common in church pronouncements until *Persona humana*.

The second aspect of the church documents of interest to us here is that of the language or wording used to delineate, "name" or restrict the various persons, actions, or categories to be identified. In general, the language used for such purposes is negative and unfailingly judgmental. Such connotations are rendered by words such as "error," "pathological," "intrinsically disordered," "distorted," and "self-indulgent." Much of the language used—frequently couched between admonitions of charity and chastity—might be seen as redolent of the more directly homophobic writings of earlier generations.

We may note here that the documentation from these pastoral sources extensively use exclusive language. But among all the words in these documents, one in particular stands out to indicate the attitudes and framework of the bishops and church authorities. This word is **homosexual**. The German term **homosexualität** can be traced at least to the late 1800s,[6] while the English term **homosexual** is first found in usage as late as 1891.[7] Regardless of when the term was actually coined, it did not become commonly used until the 1930s when it replaced such archaic terms as **sodomite, homogenic** and **invert**. The term homosexual has been utilized as a polarity *vis-à-vis* **heterosexual** in the writings of psychologists and clinical specialists. More importantly, the term is highly inexact since the term "homosexual" is depictive of actions but necessarily of identity, character or personhood. That is, a person could engage in homosexual activities but yet be constitutionally not "homosexual."[8]

On the other hand, the term **gay** antedates the other term by several centuries, possibly even as far as the sixteenth century.[9] In the late 1970s and early 1980s persons of the same-sex preference reclaimed a historically-based term for self-identification: **gay**. This term is significantly older in usage than the term "homosexual." The use of the term "gay" is primarily a self-assigned term which connotes the acceptance by an individual of his/her sexual and erotic preferences, as well as other pertinent life-choices. For gay women, the accepted term, **lesbian**, has additional historical roots in the women's colony in the age of Sappho the poetess. In both cases, the term of preference is that which is not imposed from outside, especially not from oppositional power structures, whether religious, political, moral or social.[10]

The documents of the Roman Catholic Church generally avoid using the term "gay." However some ecclesiastical leaders regard the term "homosexual" as an incorrect term of usage, since it tends to relegate the person to the sexual component of his/her personality only. Therefore, according to the argument, the term robs the person of the richness inherent in an individual personality.[11] On the other hand the term "gay" is the appellation of choice for those whose sexual orientation is toward those of the same gender. Since it is a term which is self-assigned, the term is acceptable as a name of choice. But more importantly, gay women and men look upon the word "gay" as pertaining to a whole array of life choices, attitudes, behaviors, and beliefs, all of which stem from or pertain to their affectional orientation. Thus, for many men and women the term "gay" satisfies the question which Church authorities so correctly pose about the term "homosexual."

The fact that church documents avoid the term "gay" is indicative of several possible motivations. One possible reason is that the use of the term "homosexual" is still the term of (subconscious?) choice of homophobic institutions, serving as a term which is manifestly discriminatory against people with an alternative sexual orientation.

A second possibility is that the term "gay" is not willingly released by a group of people who may see the term as being "abused" by a sexual minority, and thus is an affront to the "straight" population. Another possible reason is that the term "gay" is a power-word which tends to unite people of alternative sexual orientation thereby giving identity and unity to formerly hidden or "closeted" individuals. As a result, the majority population may view the term as potentially threatening. However, for whatever reason(s) the Church does not use the word in its documents, such neglect or oversight is indicative of the insensitivity existing in many of the documents under discussion.

(ii) Official Documents from the Vatican and the United States

The documents included in this section were chosen to give a view of the Roman Catholic magisterium from 1975 to 1986. The documents include two Vatican documents and several American pastoral statements and letters which respond within the parameters and context established by the Vatican declarations.[12]

A. Persona humana (1975): This document, dated December 29, 1975, was a public restatement of principle stated two years earlier in a 1973 guide to confessors concerning questions of homosexuality. Since it is the fundamental document in the present discussion, we shall examine it at some length.

The general tone of this public document, *Persona humana*, is presented in the very first section:

> *It is from sex that the human person receives the characteristics which . . . make that person a man or a woman, and . . . condition [the] progress toward maturity and insertion into society.*[13]

From the document's outset, it seems that a whole different

attitude conditions the stance towards sexuality than in previous documents. The social sciences, emphasized in Vatican II's *Gaudium et spes (Dogmatic Constitution on the Church in the Modern World)*, seem to have at last infiltrated the Vatican's theological work.

However, compare that uplifting opening section with the very next paragraph:

> *One of the most serious indications of this corruption (of morals) is the unbridled exaltation of sex . . . invading the field of education and infecting the general morality.*[14]

Immediately we are presented with a dilemma which faces the post-Vatican II Church: that of reconciling traditional ecclesiastical doctrine and world-views with the contributions of modern society. Just as the document, *Gaudium et spes* was filled with such tensions and uncertainties, so too is *Persona humana* filled with similar ambiguities and dualistic tendencies.

The core of this teaching document is that the Church's sexual ethic is based upon natural law. If the classical understanding of the natural law basis for ethics is to be maintained, then the explicit presupposition of this ethic is that all persons have "natural" or certain basic and essential characteristics which are shared universally with other people. These characteristics are known through reason and are conducive to specific and unchanging moral norms.[15] Such moral norms would include the classical notion of "intrinsically evil" actions which would consequently be prohibited.

The document's use of natural law is bolstered by appeals to Christian scripture and tradition. However, one such appeal is made to the "constant teaching of the magisterium" of the Church, as well as to the interpreted "moral sense of the Christian people."[16] No guidance or understanding is specified as how the "moral sense of the Christian people" is

principally derived from "authority." No guidance or understanding is specified as to how the "moral sense of the Christian people" is divined in order to enlighten the reader as to
how the *sensus fidelium* is to be recognized and implemented.[17]

The document's content discusses at length the role of
human dignity and respect for the human person. However
any alternative understanding of the interpretation of scripture or tradition is summarily termed in light of the protection which God gives the ecclesiastical Magisterium.[18] And if
there remained any doubt as to the origin of those prospects
of the natural law, *Persona humana* dismisses the contribution of culture to morality with the declaration that "principles and norms in no way owe their origin to a certain type
of culture, but rather to knowledge of the divine law and of
human nature."[19]

The document cites the traditional argument that "the
finality of the sexual act" is the ensuing value of its morality,
but that the morality of sexual relations can only be found in
the context of heterosexual marriage, especially in its openness to procreation.[20] Unmarried or "non-traditional" relationships cannot "ensure, in sincerity and fidelity, the interpersonal relationship" between two persons.[21] Homosexual
relationships exist "in opposition to the constant teaching of
the magisterium and to the moral sense of the Christian
people."[22]

However, one major pastoral distinction is made within
the document's discussion of constitutionally gay people who
must be treated

> *with understanding and sustained in the hope*
> *of overcoming their personal difficulties and*
> *their inability to fit into society. Their culp-*
> *ability will be judged with prudence.*[23]

The document goes on to say that no pastoral consideration

can or should give "moral justification" to homosexual actions, since these actions "lack an essential and indispensable finality, . . . [and] are condemned as a serious depravity." Though not all gay people "are personally responsible" for their orientation, the document nontheless maintains that "homosexual acts are intrinsically disordered and can in no case be approved of."[24]

Persona humana made a breakthrough in trying to understand and delineate the predicament of the well-intentioned gay person who is trying to "rightly-order" his/her life, that is, the person with a same-sex orientation. Because of its given premises the document resulted in a series of pastoral statements in the United States which tried to adjust the pastoral parameters to concrete situations, without simultaneously trespassing the lines which the CDF drew for the Church's pastoral praxis.

B. Pastoral Letter from Brooklyn: *The Gift of Sexuality* (1976):

About three months after the Vatican document was issued, Bishop Francis Mugavero of the Diocese of Brooklyn issued a pastoral letter, *The Gift of Sexuality*.[25] This letter dealt with similar basic themes, but the tone was substantially more pastoral. The reader is struck by the generally compassionate quality of the document: rather than stressing a series of natural law arguments, Bishop Mugavero's letter stresses the ideas of integration and relationship.

In the opening paragraph of the letter, the theme of relationship is stated. Sexuality makes us capable of loving, intimate relationships through which

> we honor God and become more like him when
> we create in our lives the loving other-centered
> relationships which at the same time give us
> such human satisfaction and personal fulfill-

ment.[26]

In vivid contrast to the earlier Vatican declaration, Mugavero states that sexuality "largely conditions his or her progress towards maturity and insertion into society."[27] This becomes a link with the theme of building responsible relationships. Mugavero is able to use this direct quote from the opening section of *Persona humana*, stipulating it as one of two qualities which are inherent in sexuality—the other being that of the capacity for relationship.

The Vatican's document's attitude toward sexuality and its appropriation is explicated at length in the document's expression of the need for "obtaining knowledge of wholesome moral teaching"[28] based on the provisions of natural law and the Christian tradition. Compare this with Mugavero's more positive tone concerning the **challenge** of sexuality:

> *The power and the pleasure which are part of sexuality will demand of us the intelligence, honesty and sacrifice that might test our maturity to the utmost degree.* **But we do not fear sexuality, we embrace it.**[29]

There is a confidence and maturity in the expression of the nature of sexuality. Corruption is a possibility, but it is not the posited given which the Vatican's statement offers. The pastoral letter not only states that we are to "embrace" sexuality as part of our life, but also that we must appreciate sexuality for its gift rather than fear concupiscence for its ability to lead us into sin. Sexuality is a positive dynamism whose quality is such that we tend to underestimate its content. Mugavero believes that our real fear resides in not thinking "as highly of the gift [of sexuality] as does God who made us sexual beings."[30]

In the title of the pastoral letter, *The Gift of Sexuality,*

Mugavero poses the problematic as to whether or not—let alone how—we view sexuality as the gratuitous gift of a gracious and loving God. Along these lines the bishop recalls that sexuality is a wholistic component of people's lives. It is not simply genitality but a means to enter the lives of others and vice-versa. "We are to follow Jesus' command to become 'lovers.' It is a relational power."[31]

Bishop Mugavero finds the ideal mode for this image in Jesus Christ, who "was fully a man—with the sexuality of a man."[32] Mugavero admits both the difficulty of integrating sexuality into life as well as the need to take conscious control over the construction of that integration. Though here marital sexuality is viewed as the norm, there is a strong positive quality which elevates Mugavero's pastoral approach above the sterility of other later documents. Mugavero acknowledges that grace is not sufficient for those who are troubled by their sexuality, though he also maintains that psychological diagnosis without grace is equally insufficient.[33] The use of modern psychology to inform this pastoral is pervasive, despite the following conclusion:

> All should strive for a sexual integration which respects that [heterosexual] norm. . . . [All people] are so much more than this single aspect of their personality. That richness must not be most.[34]

If Bishop Mugavero inevitably must reinforce the Church's teaching on the normativeness of heterosexuality, he at least attempts to call **all persons** to self-integration.

The problem which arises is that Mugavero's previously-cited statement collides with the integrative image of sexuality he presents at the beginning of his pastoral letter. Whereas in his conclusion he calls on people to avoid identifying personhood with sexual orientation, it is that very quality of sexuality which he had earlier identified as "a relational power."[35]   Were one to relate a loving, warm and compassionate manner to others, one would, according to his argument, need to treat personal sexuality in a dualistic manner: express sexuality in a relational manner while avoiding self-identification—particularly, if not exclusively, as a homosexual man or woman. This seems to contravene the integrative approach which he presents as normative throughout the pastoral letter. However, the letter is an attempt to place sexuality in relational, integrative and pastoral contexts rather than to simply view sexuality as a series of right or wrong actions.

C. Three Documents from 1983-1984:

Within the spirit and tone of the letter of Bishop Mugavero is the 1983 *Rationale for Welcoming the National Dignity Convention to Seattle* of Archbishop Raymond Hunthausen of Seattle. Writing from a spirit of dialogue with the gay community, Hunthausen recalls that a number of American dioceses had instituted special ministries to the gay Catholic populations, or had at least issued pastoral letters on the subject of homosexuality and religious affiliation.

Hunthausen echoes a theme from the 1976 American bishops' pastoral letter, *To Live in Christ Jesus* that all gay women and men should be free from deprivation of human rights:

> *They have a right to respect, friendship and justice.   They should have an active role in the Christian community.*[36]

Hunthausen's citation of this statement of the American episcopal conference is simply and yet profoundly echoed in the bishop's own words: " 'Those people' ... are really **our** people."[37]   The acceptance of "those people" as "our people" underlies Hunthausen's conviction that the people of his diocese must stand with the gay community, just as Jesus "time and time again chose to minister directly to those whom society found most difficult to accept . . . he stood with them; he was one of them; he made their cause his own."[38]   The witness to Christ is a theme for Hunthausen not only in matters concerning gay Catholics but in all matters of social justice. The dilemma is, as he states so eloquently, that

> *we will never discover the right answers unless*
> *we are willing to [go] into dialogue with those*
> *who are struggling with the issue in terms of*
> *their Catholic faith.*[39]

Such an admission of Catholic uncertainty and commitment to the process of gradual revelation represents a substantially different approach than the following statement which maintains that the freedom of homosexual women and men needs to be restricted, and that needed change should not be an expansion of rights:

> *Rights should be limited whenever they come*
> *into conflict with the rights of others and the*
> *common good. . . . What we need is education*
> *and a change of heart.*[40]

This statement from the Massachusetts Catholic Conference was a response of six bishops to a proposed state-wide anti-discrimination bill, focusing on sexual preference. Though the episcopal statement responds to the very real intricacies of rights and conflicting legal issues, this letter was couched in language which recalled the need to respond to the common good as the highest value, despite the obvious need for individual protection under the law. Education and "metanoia" (change of heart) were to be preferred to "ill-advised" laws. .

The bishops saw the need for such legislation in a far different light than they had in the past for racial, religious and/or ethnic minorities. Had it been proposed for one of these groups, it is doubtful that the bishops would have admonished people to become "educated"—by whom, and in what manner?—or experience "a change of heart" rather than seek redress of grievances. It is also doubtful that rights of heterosexuals would ever be phrased as coming into conflict with the rights of "others" or with the common good of society.

One final contemporary statement speaks for itself:

> [The homosexuals'] hearts are darkened, and God allows them to fall into immoral practices .... [They] should seek spiritual and professional counseling in order to overcome homosexuality, if possible, or at least to hold it in check.[41]

This letter, the pastoral letter of Bishop Stanislaus Brzana of Ogdensburg (New York), is redolent of all the latent, unexpressed attitudes, precariously supported by uncritical scriptural interpretation, as well as being overly-concerned with genital behavior. As seen from this brief quote, the "pastoral" letter demonstrates the persistent lack of informed perspective in episcopal leadership circles.

D. The Pastoral Care of Homosexual Persons

Though a declaration on homosexuality had been expected for some time, its issuance in 1986 nonetheless provoked dismay from both gay activists and many leading theologians, among others. No person would have reasonably expected that the Roman Catholic Church would have significantly compromised its position on same-sex affectivity. But the document was expected to have at least preserved the status quo set forth by *Persona humana*: that position would hold that, though homosexual activity was "intrinsically disordered," those who are homosexually-oriented would be considered as suffering at most from "a lack of normal sexual development."[42]

The opening page of the document states that the Church's position allows it

> to be confident that her more global vision
> does greater justice to the rich reality of the
> human person in his spiritual and physical
> dimensions created by God and heir, by grace,
> to eternal life.[43]

The Church's teaching authority maintains that the core of truth is to be found in the "more global vision" of the Church. Therefore the directives of the teaching mission of the Church must conform to the same tools cited in earlier documents—natural law and Christian tradition.

The "intrinsic disorder" of homosexual actions is maintained, but now the CDF, using scriptural citations, desires to restate its position on homosexual orientation. The CDF had perceived a neutralization of homosexuality by theologians and pastoral ministers:

> The particular inclination of the homosexual
> person [is] a more or less strong tendency
> ordered toward an intrinsic moral evil and ...
> must be seen as an objective disorder.[44]

Terming homosexual behavior as a form of "the blindness which has overcome humankind,"[45] the writers of the document proceed to term the homosexual relationship as incapable of becoming "a complementary union able to transmit life."[46]

> This does not mean that homosexual persons

> *are not often generous and giving of themselves
> .... [but] they confirm within themselves a dis-
> ordered sexual inclination which is essentially
> self-indulgent.*[47]

The authors of this document do not explain how a person
who is "objectively disordered" can possibly be "generous
and giving of oneself," nor is there any explanation for why a
homosexual action is necessarily and essentially self-indulgent. If the implication is that a selfless sexual action is one
which is "able to transmit life," how can any sexual act by a
sterile or aged couple be considered anything other than
"self-indulgent"?

The problem of orientation in relation to activity is not
dealt with, even within a scholastic framework to give cred-
ence to the axiom: *"agere sequitur esse"* (action follows being). The document avoids these questions, and it does not
explain how acts can be separated from the persons who perform these actions. As a result the document avoids a personalist ethical concern about the moral stance of the individual prior to some act's commission.

Complaints in the document concerning "enormous pres-
sure" being brought upon the Church within,[48] seem petty
in the context of the document from an institution which has
seen two thousand years of turmoil, war and schism.

> *One tactic used [by gay activists] is to protest
> that any and all criticism of or reservations
> about homosexual people, their activity and
> lifestyle are simply diverse forms of unjust dis-
> crimination.*[49]

The authors of the document discount the possibility that
the Church's own words might lead to discrimination. The
onus for discriminatory behavior is placed on the shoulders
of gay people themselves due to four different causes. First

of all, homosexual behavior is blamed since it "may seriously threaten the lives and well-being of a large number of people."[50] No distinction is made between responsible and irresponsible behavior since all homosexual behavior is considered wrong.

Secondly, the effects of prejudice stem from the reaction to the "deceitful propaganda" which the "pro-homosexual movement" issues concerning the role of the Church. Also, the view that homosexual activity is equivalent to conjugal love creates a reaction from those who understand and prize "the nature and rights of the family."[51]

Finally, the document treats violence against gay people in the following well-publicized excerpt:

> Neither the church nor society at large should be surprised when other distorted notions and practices gain ground, and irrational and violent reactions increase.[52]

This statement does not consider the historical reality of violence committed against gay people.[53] The document states that present-day violence is to be expected whenever gay people acknowledge themselves as different and demand fair treatment from society. It attempts to both condemn violence while yet maintaining that homophobic violence is understandable.

The final paragraphs of the CDF document call homosexual individuals to self-denial. The document urges them to conform by self-denial which, with the sacrifice of Christ, would constitute for them "a source of self-giving which will save them from a [self-destructive] way of life."[54] This is a natural outgrowth from the entire preceding content of the document, and is complemented by admonitions to bishops to present the teachings of the Church as Rome has interpreted it, as well as to develop compatible catechetical and educational standards.[55] The bishops are instructed to ensure that

no support—whether financial, environmental or emotional—
be given to any group which seeks to undermine the teaching
of the Church in this regard.[56]

(iii) Documents from Official Task Forces and Committees

This section is devoted to statements of four church-
sponsored task forces and/or committees. These statements
are samples of serious alternative thinking being done at various levels of the Church's structure.

A. The CTSA Study—*Human Sexuality*:

In June of 1976, the Catholic Theological Society of
America authorized the publication of the book, *Human Sexuality: New Directions in American Catholic Thought.* This
text was the product of a committee comprised of five prominent American theologians.[57]

The committee attempted to integrate material from
scripture, Christian tradition and the empirical sciences into
what they termed a "theology of human sexuality that
speaks to contemporary experience."[58] The starting point
for the committee was the prioritized procreative aspect of
sexuality and marriage as stated in Vatican II which in the
committee's words suggested that

> *the human person [be] the integrating prin-
> ciple that could harmonize both the procrea-
> tive and unitive purposes of sexuality and
> marriage . . . affirming that the values they
> represent must be expressed in the lives of all
> people, not just the married.*[59]

This was a daring approach since all the previous documents
had insisted that the procreative and unitive aspects of sexuality were ultimately only achieveable within the confines of

marriage. The committees acknowledged its debt to *Persona humana* for its recognition of sexuality as that which gives the individual his/her individual traits, something "at the foundation of . . . a new translation of the traditional Christian values which govern sexual conduct."[60]

The committee attempted to broaden the basis for the definition and meaning of sexuality. It defined sexuality as

> the way of being in, and relating to, the world as a male or female person . . . the mode or manner by which we humans experience and express our incompleteness and relatedness to each other. Human sexuality is the concrete manifestation of the divine call to completion, a call extended to every person and rooted in the very core of our being.[61]

In order to carry out this definition of sexuality as a call to completeness, the terminology of the dual aspects of sexual relations had to be replaced by the more all-encompassing terms of **creativity** and **integration**. Here wholistic sexuality is no longer only that which is expressive of openness to procreation and is unitive through the marriage bond. Rather wholistic sexuality is now to be realized by that which fosters "creative growth toward integration." This eliminates any possible conceptualization of sexuality as genitality or as exclusively physical generativity.[62]

In making the terminology broader and more encompassing, the authors of *Human Sexuality* were attempting to find theological and philosophical room for every person: all are called to creative growth through the process of integration, which the authors view "as a legitimate development of the traditional formulation" of Catholic moral teaching.[63] This broadened horizon is not a call to sexual license since the authors recognize that situations exist in which sexual actions and behvaiors may be evil, dishonest and even destructive (*e.g.*, rape, etc.).

To be conducive to creative growth and integration, sexual behavior and actions must be "self-liberating, other-enriching, honest, faithful, socially responsible, life-serving, and joyous." Abstract principles are not determinative of an action's morality or immorality. Rather, principles of action must be viewed within the context of "the persons involved, their lives, their intentions, and the personal and social consequences of their acts."[64]

Such a perspective on sexuality as in moral ethics of any kind retreats from traditional legalistic and ontic categories in favor of ontological, experiential and personalist contexts. Many theologians and ethicists are uncomfortable with what they would call "relativists." Rather than being relativistic the authors' approach is within the context of personalism. But the main thrust is to see morality and sexuality as an integrative principle from within the human person (ontological), rather than being imposed from outside the person (ontic).

The personalist view of scripture and tradition reflects a theological pluralism which the authors see as already existing in the Church:

> *Catholic tradition is richer, broader and more complex than most realize. For that reason Catholic moral teaching is more diverse than most people realize.*[65]

In trying to be faithful to the spirit of Catholic teaching via the gospels and tradition, the CTSA study raised a number of objections from some theologians, from the Church hierarchy and even from the Vatican itself. But the CTSA committee's bold person-oriented stance made a dramatic contribution to the broadening and deepening of the theology of sexuality.

B. The Baltimore and San Francisco Task Force on Gays and Lesbians

An innovative measure taken up by the archbishops of Baltimore and San Francisco, William Borders and John Quinn, was the creation of "task forces" on the questions concerning ministry to and on behalf of gay and lesbian persons. Each task force issued a rationale for such a ministry.

The Baltimore Task Force issued its brief statement on October 5, 1981. Its clear pronouncement is that a clearly-defined ministry to gays and lesbians is needed "to bear witness to [the archdiocese's] opposition to the injustice they have suffered and are suffering."[66] Society is the main locus for the rendered injustices. However, the church is also a source of injustices, "such as the denial of respect and of full participation in the community."[67]

Though refraining from making moral pronouncements as its central purpose, the task force reminds gay people that the starting point for all sexual integration is Christ's call to perfection:

> It entails living out the demands of chastity within that orientation . . . [informed by a properly-informed] conscience. . . [integrating] the "Christian principles inherent in the truths that Christ revealed."[68]

This document maintains the ideal of chastity even though the individual well-informed conscience still seems to be the main arbiter. This document is an example of the type of statement which the 1986 Vatican declaration condemned as ambiguous and needing correction.[69]

The lengthy San Francisco task force document is not nearly as nuanced or as restrained as the relatively brief Baltimore statement. The fifty-four recommendations of the committee were direct and unsparing in their language and purpose. For our study only a brief portion of this work will be examined.

In the introduction to the final report, entitled *Homosexuality and Social Justice*, the theme of the title is sounded out in a graphic account of a brutal attack upon a gay man in 1981, not only decrying the violence but also condemning the institutional maltreatment of the victim. The righteous anger inherent in this account permeates the entire document. Numerous accounts by lesbians and gay men recount the multitude of injustices perpetrated by an unjust society. But one organization in particular is specifically targeted for criticism: the Roman Catholic Church.

The content of this report is a criticism of sexual discrimination, disenfranchisement, ostracism, etc. But above all the report is an account of the journey of gay men and women who call themselves Roman Catholic. Ironically the unique quality of this task force report is that it was officially sponsored by the Archdiocese of San Francisco and that a majority of the committee members were gay Roman Catholics. It is not surprising that soon after the report was published the task force was officially disbanded.

C. The Statement of the Washington State Catholic Conference

The remarkable document, *The Prejudice against Homosexuals and the Ministry of the Church*, was a product of the Washington State Catholic Conference. Given its provenance it is not surprising that this document is so pastoral in its tone. What is truly remarkable is its frank language concerning the Church's role in the eradication or preservation of prejudice toward lesbians and gay men in Church and society.

The language of the document easily accommodates the terms **gay** and **lesbian**, unlike so many earlier statements. The statement clearly states that "the teaching itself, at times, has

been expressed in a way that has occasioned prejudicial attitudes and activity on the part of some Church members."[70]

Prejudice, in general, falls short of the norm for all Christian morality, and thus, prejudice must be combatted at all
times. But an even greater infringement of the norm is prejudice against gays and lesbians due not only to their actions
but even to their very orientation as gay people.[71] This prejudice impedes their growth and development. Since Catholics have heard the Church's teaching on homosexuality
within an already-biased society, the prejudice is compound-
ed:

> As a result they [society's actions and atti-
> tudes] have given to the Church's teaching a
> nuance which is prejudicial to homosexual
> persons.[72]

Because of this the Church has a serious obligation with regards to eradicating prejudice toward gay women and men.

The document enumerates the responsibilities of Church
and State toward gay people. Among these responsibilities
are that the State must guarantee against discriminatory practices, against unreasonable invasion of sexual privacy, and
against infringement of rights within the workplace. Both
Church and State must protect gay persons from discrimination stemming from biased attitudes, and both must guarantee the humane public treatment of gay persons by safe-
guarding those basic rights which all others enjoy.[73]

The truly challenging section of this statement comes in
the section on rectifying prejudicial situations and attitudes
in the Church itself. Not only should the Church eliminate
the way it communicates prejudicial attitudes, but it is also
"obligated to combat [them] by fostering ongoing theological research and criticism, with regard to its own theological
tradition(s)...none of which is infallibly taught."[74] Such recommendations as these were similar to those found by the

San Francisco task force. But since the WSCC was sponsored by the hierarchy for the church in the state of Washington, the impact of these recommendations was even more pronounced than those in San Francisco. For in Washington those with authority were making the statement, while those in San Francisco eventually lost all official sponsorship.

(iv) Conclusion

We have sampled several pastoral documents concerning gay people. In doing so, we have seen that a variety of thought exists, despite the efforts of Vatican authorities to standardize doctrinal thought.

It is clear that a variety of efforts by bishops and laity has attempted to implement these Vatican pronouncements while yet recognizing the expectations of different sectors of the American church. No episcopal pastoral letter has defied the Vatican parameters, though some have "stretched" the officially-drawn lines and, unfortunately, other documents have been issued which have concretized what was intended by earlier ones.

The Vatican-influenced documents do not reflect the dialogical or democratic foundations which are part of the American experience. As a result active resistance to such authoritarian statements does arise. However, there still exists within American Catholics the desire to be a faithful part of the transactional institution which has been part of their heritage as Catholics.

There is something inherent in Catholicism which runs counter to the traditional notion of the American "redeemer nation."[75] The trans-national versus the super-national: the ambivalence of Catholics to this tension runs deep. The question of how to be simultaneously both a good Catholic and a loyal American has plagued many generations of American Catholics, but in the 1980s they have realized that there is no need for any such contradiction. Today's American Catholic laity now listens with a fuller awareness and a healthy skepticism, cognizant of both one's obligations and rights in light of the Church's past.

When the American gay Catholic listens to the Church's authoritarian words concerning his/her morality, the recollection of the Church's past teaching touches painful memories. But because of the American heritage of the struggle for human and civil rights, the gay person recognizes those same words as oppressive and archaic. It is no wonder that the American Catholic gay individual experiences a profound love-hate relationship with the Church. To that person the Church is both mother and keeper, loving and neutering, the incarnation of divine freedom as well as the embodiment of oppression.

—**Craig Wesley Pilant, Ph.D. (candidate)**

NOTES

[1] It is important to state that even the most liberal of American bishops themselves did not exceed the boundaries of that earlier Vatican document. However, several episcopally-sponsored or selected task-forces and committees did so through their observations and recommendations.

[2] Timothy E. O'Connell, *Principles for a Catholic Morality* (San Francisco: Harper and Row, 1976), p. 166.

[3] Philip S. Keane, *Sexual Morality: A Catholic Perspective* (New York: Paulist Press, 1977), pp. 47-49.

[4] O'Connell, *Principles for a Catholic Morality*, pp. 166-168.

[5] Karl Barth, quoted in Edward J. Batchelor (ed.), *Homosexuality and Ethics* (New York: Pilgrim Press, 1980), p. 49.

[6] John Boswell, *Christianity, Social Tolerance and Homosexuality: Gay People in Western Europe from the Beginning of the Christian Era to the Fourteenth Century* (Chicago University of Chicago Press, 1980), pp. 42-43.

[7] *Ibid.*, p. 42, no. 4.

[8] *Ibid.*, p. 44.

[9] *Ibid.*, p. 43, n. 6.

[10] Toby Marotta, *The Politics of Homosexuality* (Boston: Houghlin-Mifflin Co., 1981), p. 91.

[11] John Gallagher (ed.), *Homosexuality and the Magisterium: Documents from the Vatican and U.S. Bishops, 1975-1985* (Mt. Rainier, MD: New Ways Ministry, 1986), p. 85.

[12] Citations from the Vatican documents refer to section and paragraph numbers. Citations for the American pastoral documents refer to their publication within *Origins* in John Gallagher's *Homosexuality and the Magisterium.*

[13] Sacred Congregation for the Doctrine of the Faith. *Persona humana: The Vatican Declaration on Sexual Ethics, Origins* 5:31 (January 22, 1976), 1.1.

[14] *Ibid.*, 1.2.

[15] Lisa Sowie Cahill, *Between the Sexes: Foundations for a Christian Ethics of Sexuality* (Philadelphia: Fortress Press, 1983), p. 79.

[16] *Persona humana*, 8.1.

[17] Richard P. McBrien, *Catholicism* (Minneapolis, MN:

[18] *Persona humana*, 4.1-3.

[19] *Ibid.*, 5.1.

[20] *Ibid.*, 5.5-6.

[21] *Ibid.*, 7.2.

[22] *Ibid.*, 8.1.

[23] *Ibid.*, 8.2-4.

[24] *Ibid.*, 8.4.

[25] Dated February 11, 1976.

[26] Francis J. Mugavero, "The Gift of Sexuality," *Origins* 5:37 (March 4, 1976), p. 581.

[27] *Idem.*

[28] *Persona humana*, 2.1.

[29] Mugavero, "The Gift of Sexuality," p. 583 (emphasis added.)

[30] *Idem.*

[31] *Idem.*

[32] *Idem.*

[33] *Ibid.*, p. 584.

[34] *Ibid.*, p. 585.

[35] *Ibid.*, p. 583.

[36] Gallagher, *op. cit.*, p. 81.

[37] *Idem.*

[38] *Ibid.*, p. 82.

[39] *Idem.*

[40] *Ibid.*, p. 99.

[41] *Ibid.*, pp. 92-93.

[42] *Persona humana*, 8.2-4.

[43] Sacred Congregation for the Doctrine of the Faith, "Letter to the World's Bishops on the Pastoral Care of Homosexual Persons," *Origins* 16:22 (November 13, 1986), 2:1-2.

[44] *Ibid.*, p. 3:2.

[45] *Ibid.*, 6.4.

[46] *Ibid.*, 7.2.

[47] *Ibid.*, 3.2.

[48] *Ibid.*, 8.2-9.2.

[49] *Ibid.*, 9:1.

[50] *Ibid.*, 9:2.

[51] *Ibid.*, 9:3.

[52] *Ibid.*, 10.1-2.

[53] Commission on Social Justice, Archdiocese of San Francisco, *Homosexuality and Social Justice ; Report of the Task Force on Gay/Lesbian Issues, July 1982* (San Francisco: Archdiocese of San Francisco, 1982), pp. 17-26.

[54] "The Pastoral Care of Homosexual Persons," 12:4.

[55] *Ibid.*, 14:1, 17:3-6.

[56] *Ibid.*, 15.1, 17:8.

[57] Anthony Kosnick, William Carroll, Agnes Cunningham, Ronald Modras, and James Schulte, *Human Sexuality: New Directions in American Catholic Thought* (New York: Paulist Press, 1976).

[58] *Ibid.*, p. 92.

[59] *Idem.*

[60] *Ibid.*, p. 93.

[61] *Idem.*

[62] *Idem.*

[63] *Ibid.*, p. 86.

[64] *Ibid.*, p. 93.

[65] *Idem.*

[66] Baltimore Archdiocesean Task Force, "Baltimore's Ministry to Lesbian and Gay Catholics," *Origins*, 11.35

(February 11, 1982), p. 551.

[67] *Idem.*

[68] *Ibid.*, p. 552.

[69] "The Pastoral Care of Homosexual Persons," 3:2.

[70] Gallagher, *op. cit.*, p. 46.

[71] *Ibid.*, pp. 49-50.

[72] *Ibid.*, p. 50.

[73] *Ibid.*, pp. 52-53.

[74] *Ibid.*, pp. 53-54.

[75] Cf. Ernest Tuveson, *Redeemer Nation: The Idea of America's Millennial Role* (Chicago: University of Chicago Press, 1968).

The AIDS Crisis:
Legitimation of Homophobia or Catalyst for Change?

(i) Introduction

Gay persons with AIDS (PWAs) confront traditional religious institutions with a "dilemma of status."[1]   On the one hand, as sick persons, PWAs evoke care from religious organizations.   On the other, homosexual acts have been the object of strong religious proscriptions. I will examine what effect, if any, the presence of AIDS in the gay community has had on anti-gay behavior and attitudes expressed by one traditional religious institution—the Roman Catholic Church in the United States.

John Seidler[2] maintains that the changes occuring within Roman Catholicism since Vatican II have been the result of social forces within the Church as well as outside it. Yet, these changes have been fought by forces of counter-modernization.   He calls this movement toward change "contested accommodation." Conflict, he argues, initiates reform. Seidler mentions the shift toward democratic structures within the Church as an example of such change. Priests and laity have gained a degree of organizational power through their participation in priests' senates and parish councils. Yet counter-modernizing forces in positions of power (e.g., the Vatican Curial) have resisted change, resulting in only a slight movement toward democratic structures within the Church.

Seidler maintains that change occurs in different segments of the Church at different times. While the inertia of the institution favors the status quo, the social environment, key events or prophetic personalities all may turn the tide in bringing about institutional reform. While Roman Catholicism has changed a great deal from the days before the Second Vatican Council, sexual morality has certainly not been an area where change has occurred within the Church on the official level. However, groups both within the Church and without have clamored for change in official teachings concerning issues such as birth control, abortion and homosexuality. The AIDS crisis has the potential to act as a variable adding momentum to the forces of change, or alternatively, reinforcing the status quo.

In the context of this discussion two problematic terms have already emerged: **'homosexual'** and **'homophobia'**. The medical term 'homosexual' appeared in the nineteenth century and soon replaced the religiously inspired term 'sodomite' in general usage.[3] Social elites, such as the medical establishment, defined 'homosexuality' as both a social problem and a disease. As John Boswell[4] notes: " 'homosexual' defines a person only in terms of his/her sexuality. The term 'homosexuality' also refers to acts engaged in by any person with a member of the same sex."

The term **'gay,'** however, was coined by gay people in the context of the struggle for gay liberation. Jim Cotter[5] states that the term 'gay' is "a sign in the world that some people are creating their own identity in a society that has, on the whole, refused to allow them to exist openly and unafraid." Also, 'gay is often accepted by lesbians as well as gay men. In this paper, I use the term 'homosexual' in the context of quotations from other sources, or when I discuss the views of Church leaders who define gay people either by their sexual acts or 'deviant' orientation.

'Homophobia' is another problematic term. While Boswell[6] notes its linguistic difficulties,[7] the word poses more substantive problems. First, having a phobia of something often means one will avoid the object of that fear. However, many societal attitudes and behaviors generally understood as homophobic are directed toward gay people and do not represent attempts to avoid them.[8] **'Homophobia'** is also a medicalization of anti-gay attitudes and behavior, removing the onus from the victimizers by defining them as sick. Therefore, while I generally use the term 'anti-gay,' some attitudes and behaviors I discuss are 'homophobic,' in the sense that they are mechanisms for avoiding gay persons and gay sexuality, especially when embodied in PWAs.

(ii) AIDS and Ecclesiastical Response

I discuss the responses of Church hierarchy by examining official documents that deal with both homosexuality and AIDS. In an effort to understand how these official statements play themselves out in actual ministry to PWAs, I also examine the attitudes of priests involved in AIDS ministry. This data comes from interviews I have conducted with 32 priests in the Archdiocese of Los Angeles who have expressed a willingness to minister to PWAs. All but five of these priests have actually ministered to PWAs.

(A) Hierarchy

The Vatican has made a thinly disguised reference to AIDS in a statement on homosexuality:

> *Even when the practice of homosexuality may seriously threaten the lives and wellbeing of a large number of people, its advocates remain undeterred and refuse to consider the magnitude of the risks involved.*[9]

From this perspective, AIDS is directly related to homosexual acts. This response is a case of "blaming the victim" for contracting the disease.

Since the Vatican asserts that homosexuality itself is a threat to life and health, the Church cannot endorse laws which protect the civil rights of homosexuals. When governments enact gay rights laws, the letter continues, violence against homosexuals should not be surprising.[10] From this perspective, both AIDS and violent societal reactions toward gays are examples of the chaos that ensues when individuals or societies violate the natural law. AIDS and anti-gay violence are held up as a legitimation of allegedly immutable moral norms.

Homosexuals should receive the respect and dignity due all human persons, the Vatican maintains. Nevertheless, homosexuals are seen as intrinsically disordered and dysfunctional. The Vatican states that homosexual persons are worthy of pastoral care and counseling because of their "disorder," but leaves the question of the morality of any gay sexual relationships unexamined, since the immorality of homosexual acts is assumed *a priori* in the Church's "constant Tradition."[11]

John Harvey, a strong advocate of the Vatican's anti-gay position, teases out some of the details only briefly mentioned in the letter cited above. Harvey maintains that even apart from AIDS, homosexual activity is unhealthy. He states:

> *From a theological point of view I would add that it [homosexual sex] is a violation of the human body and of the plan of the Creator for the procreation of the human race, as well as a parody of true marital love.*[12]

AIDS, he asserts, only further legitimates the Church's teaching concerning homosexual acts. Harvey is not as extreme as fundamentalists such as Jerry Falwell,[13] who see AIDS as a direct punishment of God. Still, Harvey sees PWAs as receiving the unfortunate desserts of their 'sinful' lifestyles. While Harvey advocates Church involvement in care for PWAs, he notes the need for priests to uphold the Church's objective moral teaching when ministering to PWAs.[14]

Other hierarchical responses express concern for the sick and deemphasize the 'sinful' lifestyle of PWAs. When Pope John Paul II spoke to PWAs at Mission Dolores Basilica in San Francisco in September of 1987, he emphasized the

Church's care for all those who are ill. Noting that God's love is embodied in the Church, the Pope went on to say:

> God loves all without distinction and without
> limit. . . . He loves those of you who are sick,
> those suffering from AIDS and AIDS-related
> complex.

While the Pope concentrated on God's love and acceptance, he began his address by noting that God's love calls all people to repentence of sin and to coversion. Even though stated in very general terms, the pope's message was certainly intended to call gay PWAs to repent of their lifestyle.

A statement from the Bishops of California is another example of the Church's emphasis on the care of the sick. Here, even less attention is paid to questions of 'sinful' sexual acts. The statement encourages Catholics to educate themselves about the disease to dispel irrational fears of AIDS. It also notes PWA's needs for practical assistance and companionship. In one paragraph devoted to "Special concerns for homosexual persons" the bishops state:

> The most obvious high risk individuals still con-
> tinue to be members of the homosexual com-
> munity, some of whom have been separated
> from the Church and its spiritual life. We regret
> this distance, and long to heal their wounds by
> offering our support and fellowship.[15]

This statement does not mention the Church's condemnation of all gay sexual relationships as intrinsically evil. It focuses on the care of the sick and reconciliation of gays with the Church. Whether this statement is a movement toward a dialogue on the Church's moral teaching remains unclear.

Another episcopal letter, from the Administrative Board of the United States Catholic Conference, discusses the

Church's response to the AIDS crisis in more detail. The statement condemns discrimination against PWAs and calls for a response of compassion toward the sick. The Bishops state further:

> *We are alarmed by the increase of negative atti-*
> *tudes as well as acts of violence directed against*
> *gay and lesbian people since AIDS became a*
> *national issue. Those who are gay or lesbian or*
> *suffering from AIDS should not be the objects*
> *of discrimination, injustice or violence.*[16]

The Bishops do not encourage or support anti-gay violence and indeed call for an end to violence against homosexuals. At the same time, they do not advocate any positive action to ensure justice toward gays (*e.g.*, gay rights legislation).

An early portion of the statement follows John Paul II's remarks in calling for repentance of sin:

> *Jesus also proclaimed to those most in need the*
> *good news of forgiveness. The father in the*
> *parable did not wait for his son to come to*
> *him. Rather, he took the initiative and ran out*
> *to his son with generosity, forgiveness and*
> *compassion. This spirit of forgiveness Jesus*
> *handed on to his followers.*[17]

The Bishops speak of forgiveness and acceptance in general, but clearly they believe gays, along with drug abusers, need to repent of their lifestyle.

In discussing preventive AIDS education, the bishops strongly uphold the official proscription on all homosexual activity. While the statement allowed the possibility of discussing condom use in the context of AIDS education seminars, even this pastoral concession became a hotly contested issue among the American bishops. Archbishop Roger Mahony of the Archdiocese of Los Angeles,[18] for example, noted that the Bishops' statements on preventive education should not be understood as a "shift in the constant moral teaching of the Catholic Church."[19] Indeed, the revised version of the document, accepted in November 1989 by the Bishops of the United States, deleted the sections which allowed for discussion of condom use in AIDS education programs. The bishops deleted the controversial portions of the document, rather than give the impression that the Church's views on sexuality are changeable. Even in the earlier draft of the letter written by the administrative board, the Bishops assert:

> Human sexuality is essentially related to permanent commitment in love and openness to new life. It is most fully realized when it is expressed in a manner that is as loving, faithful and committed as is divine love itself. That is why we call upon all people to live in accord with the authentic meaning of love and sexuality. Human sexuality, as we understand this gift from God, is to be genitally expressed only in a monogamous heterosexual relationship of lasting fidelity in marriage.[20]

The statement continues that this understanding of sexuality is the only way to stop "a major source of the spread of AIDS."

Thus, the Bishops first make no distinction between gay monogamy and gay promiscuity; all sex outside of marriage is portrayed as not only immoral but unhealthy.[21] Second, only heterosexual sex reflects divine love and can be expressed through loving commitment. Third, it can be inferred from the Bishops' position that gay relationships are unauthentic, less than truly human and lacking in loving commitment. Fourth, the Bishops base their reasoning on a neo-scholastic paradigm of moral theology, in which moral laws are rigid and immutable.

However, when discussing PWAs, the Bishops move away from discussions of sexual morality and emphasize care for the sick rather than disdain for homosexual acts. In a similar vein, Cardinal John O'Connor,[22] who has stridently opposed gay civil rights legislation, criticizes charges presented by gay Catholics that the Church could not minister to gay PWAs since it condemns their lifestyle. He cites various medical care programs for PWAs in the New York Archdiocese as evidence that the Church can indeed hold its moral position and care for the sick. By separating the identity of PWAs as gay men from their identity as sick persons, O'Connor upholds a traditional ministry to the sick as well as a traditional condemnation of homosexuality.

The Administrative Board's letter maintains this separation as well. By defining PWAs only as sick persons, the Bishops feel free to call for allocation of government resources for AIDS research and patient care, and to speak out against discrimination of PWAs in housing, employment and insurance. They call for public education concerning AIDS transmission as a means of allaying fear of the disease as well as eliciting a more compassionate response toward the sick.

Responses to the AIDS crisis from Roman Catholic hierarchy, therefore, are of two main types. First, as seen in the Vatican example, the AIDS crisis is used as a legitimation of traditional proscriptions against all homosexual acts. AIDS also is said to legitimate the abridgement of gay rights since the sexual activity of gay persons is said to be socially dangerous.

A second approach, seen in the letter from the Administrative Board of the U.S. Catholic Conference of Bishops, appears more conciliatory; yet the Bishops maintain the official Church position on sexual acts. The letter masks the conflict inherent in this position. In the conciliatory passages of the letter, the Bishops generally discuss the status of homosexuals as persons deserving human dignity and decry violence and discrimination against both gays and PWAs. The Bishops appear tolerant and accepting. When stating that they regret the distance between gays and the Church, however, they give no proposal for how this distance might be bridged except through the call to repentence mentioned in the first section of the letter.

The focus of the statement is on treating PWAs as sick persons rather than as gay persons. Of course, not all PWAs are gay, and the Bishops must address this diversity. Nevertheless, in the educational passages, the Bishops focus on the sexual transmission of AIDS and briefly note other means of contracting the disease (*e.g.* intravenous drug use). In this discussion, the Bishops firmly adhere to traditional teachings of sexual morality. Thus, the focus on care and acceptance of the sick masks both the Church's rigid condemnation of all sexual expression outside heterosexual marriage and the hierarchical assertion that loving gay relationships are essentially unauthentic. This position can only be understood as an assault on the experience of gay people.

While separating AIDS from homosexuality and defining it as a disease deserving of care and compassion serves to destigmatize PWAs, this strategy helps Church officials distance themselves from the stigma of homosexuality associated with AIDS. Such a stance also allows them to avoid discussing what their position on homosexuality means for gay PWAs. Do they need repentance? Should they be condemned? Such a position can be called homophobic in that it avoids dealing with the issue of gay sexuality as it is embodied in sick persons.

(B) Priests

The AIDS crisis does not appear to have had an effect on the Church's official anti-gay position. If anything, AIDS has been used to legitimate traditional teachings. Generally, the experience of priests in AIDS ministry has not challenged beliefs they have previously held either. More liberal priests see PWAs as people who embody the dying Christ in their suffering. These priests attempt to help PWAs to accept themselves as gay persons and as Christians. As one hospital chaplain noted:

> *Catechesis is important to update people in what they learned at an earlier time in their lives and because they have become somewhat distanced from organized religion. . . . One of the main things is to relieve them and inform them about a much more correct attitude about homosexuality. I think that's a basic issue. That's simply the stuff we've gotten and a terrible misunderstanding and judgmental attitude shown to gay people are simply not based in good biblical scholarship.*

These priests did not see the Church's official teaching on homosexuality as the idea; nor did they present this teaching as authoritative in their ministry with PWAs. Rather, they discussed a more gay affirming theology and attempted to reconcile PWAs with the Church on this basis.

Yet the majority of priests believed they at least had to explain the Church's teaching on homosexuality to PWAs, if not actually try to convince PWAs of the correctness of the teaching. As one parish priest noted:

> *The positive statement the Church is trying to make in the statements [on homosexuality] is that sexuality fully has its home in a faithful, committed, married, heterosexual relationship open to the transmission of life. Sexuality fully has its home there. Anything other than that is in some way deficient. Not necessarily*

> to use that term deficient in a pejorative, guilt
> inducing, finger pointing sense, but isn't really
> quite what it should be. But then again, most
> of us live our lives in every area not really, by
> various objective standards, what they should
> be. Our lives in every aspect are lived some-
> where under the ideal.

For these priests, Church teaching was the ideal and was to
be upheld even though Catholic people never lived up to it
completely. Yet, the official teaching was something for
which Catholics should strive.[23] Heterosexual marriage was
still understood as the ideal; gay relationships were seen as
deficient. These priests attempted to reconcile the PWA with
the Church and to accept the Church's view on sexuality—at
least as an ideal.[24] They used their concern and ministry for
the PWA as a way to soft sell the official teaching.

However, a clear majority of priests noted that if an
individual PWA would not accept the Church's teaching, then
he could still be reconciled with the Church, because the
individual conscience had priority over objective teaching. As
another parish priest mentioned:

> If your conscience tells you it's right even
> though I tell you it's wrong, you are respons-
> ible to live your life. It's kind of a weasel
> approach and kind of a legalistic approach, but
> it allows me as a pastoral minister to care for
> the people without being a judge, jury and exe-
> cutioner.

From this perspective the PWA could ultimately be reconciled with the Church through the authority of the priest as the
Church's official minister.

All the priests interviewed saw PWAs primarily as sick
persons in need of ministry. As I noted above, this strategy

helps destigmatize the persons with AIDS. At the same time it allows priests to deal with their dual roles as pastors and representatives of the official church. However, this strategy also veils the identity of the PWA as a gay person, allowing pastoral ministers not to grapple with the Church's teaching as it confronts them in individual PWAs.

Both heirarchal statements on AIDS and pastoral ministry to PWAs diverts attention from the Church's official teaching on homosexuality. Such a diversion neutralizes the ability of the AIDS crisis to serve as a critique of the Church's teaching. In the United States Catholic Conference letter on AIDS (noted above), the bishops did not state that gay PWAs needed to repent of their lifestyle, although they intimated this in the first paragraph; yet this is the logical outcome of the Church's teaching. There is also no recognition that anti-gay theological positions are at least partly to blame for societal violence against gays and discrimination against PWAs. By separating the gay identity of PWAs from their identity as sick persons, both bishops and priests who uphold the traditional teaching can ignore the role the Church has played in alienating the individuals they now seek to reconcile.

(iii) Conclusion

Bishops and priests, at least those who assent to the Church's teaching, limit criticism against the Church by emphasizing reconciliation and acceptance for PWAs and for gay persons. By providing a facile reconciliation with the Church on the individual level, the Church can neutralize criticism from PWAs who were alienated from the Church.

John Seidler[25] discusses a similar phenomenon in his concept of the Church as a lazy monopoly. Like an organization which produces a product or service over which it believes it has a monopoly, the Church provides enough service to its clients to preserve the status quo. The organizational elite—the hierarchy—welcome the disaffiliation of critics who are not satisfied with the level of service provided so that the existing product remains unchallenged.

In the AIDS crisis, Church officials provide a minimum of service to deflect criticism and satisfy PWAs who ask for ministry. At the same time the hierarchy gives the impression of care and concern for the sick and even expresses concern over alienated gay people in general. However, the essential Church teaching, defining a gay lifestyle as always sinful and dysfunctional, remains intact as does the ecclesiastical power structure which holds a monopoly on the means of "legitimate" moral discourse.

Gays who do not accept the Church's teaching often leave the Church. While many gays and gay PWAs believe this is the only response they can make to an anti-gay and homophobic institution, their separation deprives the institutional Church of a valuable critique. Others remain connected to the structure via alternative gay affirming communities, which satisfy the spiritual needs of individual participants. Yet even these groups may give participants a mistaken understanding of the official Church's stance toward gay persons. Furthermore, these groups may be satisfied with their ecclesial experience and pay little heed to the wider Church or the hierarchy. As a result, the ability of these groups to act as a critical force for change is neutralized.

Nevertheless, the heirarchical response to the AIDS crisis may itself help to bring about further change in the Church in terms of grassroots militancy if not organizational reform. The Vatican letter on the pastoral care of homosexual persons, and even the United States bishops' letter on AIDS have both demonstrated that the Church has not changed its teachings on sexuality nor its methods for establishing that teaching. Additionally, in response to the Vatican's letter, many dioceses in the United States forbade gay affirming groups (such as Dignity) to meet on Church property. These official responses should serve to rouse gay affirming Catholics from any sense of complacency and enkindle resistance toward attacks against gays.

Ecclesiastical change, as I have noted above, comes only after much conflict. In light of this situation, gay affirming Catholics need to continue developing what Sharon Welch calls "communities of resistance and solidarity."[26] Through their resistance, gay affirming faith communities can critique situations and structures of oppression in the religious establishment as well as society at large. Through their experience of solidarity, gay persons find a place where their voices are heard.

A gay affirming critique of the official Church cannot simply be directed at its refusal to legitimate gay unions. Rather it needs to confront the very structures of moral discourse, in which an ecclesiastical elite holds control over the means of religious production.[27] Substantive ecclesiastical change can only occur when those affected by official Church teaching have a voice in the shaping of moral discourse. Yet these alternative voices will not find expression in the institutional Church unless they first speak through the alternative discourse of communities of solidarity. These communities therefore, can become the basis of resistance toward institutional oppression, and the source of reflection for a theology of liberation as it applies to the experience of gay people.

—Mark R. Kowalewski, Ph.D.

NOTES

[1] Everett C. Hughes, "Dilemmas and Contradictions of Status," *American Journal of Sociology* 50 (1945), pp. 353-359.

[2] John Seidler, "Contested Accommodation: The Catholic Church as a Special Case of Social Change," *Social Forces* 64 (1986), pp. 847-874.

[3] This terminological shift is an example of the general social movement from defining 'deviance' as badness to sickness. 'Homosexual' referred to one who has a sexual proclivity toward members of one's own sex. This was understood as a pathological condition. See: Peter Conrad and Joseph W. Schneider, *Deviance and Medicalization: From Badness to Sickness* (St. Louis, MO: C. V. Mosby, 1980).

[4] John Boswell, *Christianity, Social Tolerance and Homosexuality* (Chicago: University of Chicago Press, 1980), pp. 44-45.

[5] Jim Cotter, "The Gay Challenge to Traditional Notions of Homosexuality," in *Towards a Theology of Gay Liberation*, ed. Malcolm Macourt (London: SCM Press, 1977), pp. 64-65.

[6] Boswell, *op cit.*, p. 46, n. 11.

[7] Homophobia literally refers to "fear of the same," rather than "fear of homosexuals."

[8] Simon Watney, *Policing Desire* (Minneapolis, MN: University of Minnesota Press, 1987).

[9] Sacred Congregation for the Doctrine of the Faith. *Letter to the Bishops of the Catholic Church on the Pastoral Care of Homosexual Persons* (Washington, DC: United States Catholic Conference, 1986), sec. 9.

[10] *Ibid.*, sec. 10.

[11] *Ibid.*, sec. 7.

[12] John Harvey, *The Homosexual Person: New Thinking in Pastoral Care* (San Francisco: Ignatius, 1987), p. 205.

[13] Jerry Falwell, "AIDS: The Judgment of God," *Liberty Report* (April 1987), pp. 2, 5.

[14] Harvey, *op. cit.*, p. 213.

[15] California Catholic Conference, "A Call to Compassion: Pastoral Letter on AIDS to the Catholic Community of California," *Commentary* 8.4 (May 1987), unpaginated.

[16] United States Catholic Conference Administration Board, "The Many Faces of AIDS: A Gospel Response," in *Origins* 17 (1987), p. 484.

[17] *Ibid.*

[18] Archbishop John L. May, president of the NCCB, appointed Mahoney to head a redrafting committee for the statement. The committee was appointed to clarify any confusion over the Church's teaching posed by the discussion of prophylactic AIDS education.

[19] Roger Mahoney, "Statement of Clarification on 'The Many Faces of AIDS: A Gospel Response'," [unpublished statement] (December 14, 1987).

[20] United States Catholic Conference Administration Board, *op. cit.*, p. 486.

[21] This position is similar to that found later in the document: "Abstinence outside and fidelity within marriage as well as the avoidance of intravenous drug abuse are the only

morally correct and medically sure ways to prevent the spread of AIDS," *Loc cit.*, p. 486. Monogramy, per se, is not advocated, but rather marital monogamy. The bishops allege that this is a medical as well as a moral recommendation.

[22] John J. O'Connor, 1985-1986. "The Archdiocese and AIDS," *Bondings* 8.2 (Winter 1985-1986), pp. 8-9, reprinted from *Catholic New York* (September 19, 1985).

[23] Charles Curran (1984) states that this is a common pastoral practice. When counseling couples who have difficulty practicing the Church's teaching on birth control, for example, priests are to show patience and forgiveness. Curran notes that the 1980 Synod of Bishops reminded priests to use this "law of gradualness" in their pastoral ministry. Curran also holds that another acceptable practice is to allow for legitimate dissent from the Church's teaching based on the decision of a well formed conscience. Such a decision will not simply disregard the teaching, but will weigh it heavily.

[24] While stating that the official teaching was the ideal, a number of these priests believed that it would be impossible for gays to live it out. Thus, as a pastoral measure, it would be morally permissable for gays to live in monogamous relationships.

[25] John Seidler, "Priest Resignations in a Lazy Monopoly," *American Sociological Review* 44 (1979), pp. 763-783.

[26] Sharon D. Weich, *Communities of Resistance and Solidarity* (Maryknoll, NY: Orbis, 1985).

[27] See: Otto Maduro, *Religion and Social Conflicts*, trans. Robert R. Barr (Maryknoll, NY: Orbis, 1982); and, Leonardo Boff, *Church, Charism and Power* (New York: Crossroad, 1985).

Fear and Passion:
A Psychological Reflection on the Construction of
Homophobia in the Context of AIDS

Opinions and attitudes regarding Acquired Immune Deficiency Virus (AIDS) are informed and nourished by sources which are not dependent upon the epidemiological and medical reality of AIDS as much as on the homophobic mythology which precedes and embelishes a popular understanding of AIDS.[1] These attitudes have historically informed civil law, psychiatry and medicine, while they are themselves informed by a past that is so distant as to fade into anamnesis.[2]

The sources which inform many popular attitudes about AIDS have something to do with prevailing and pre-existing attitudes concerning homosexuality, and some features of this tendency can be illustrated through an examination of the anti-homosexual and ultimately homophobic trends of Christianity in the modern context of AIDS. Two questions emerge which abbreviate a theoretical approach substantially: Are people homophobic because homosexuality is dangerous? And, is homosexuality itself experienced as perilous because of the way it is perceived in cultural and religious contexts?

The irrational roots of a phobic attitude toward gay experience are problematic. There is, for example, a widespread resistance to information about AIDS, and a phobic position seems to remain intact[3] regardless of sophisticated advertising and educational campaigns. To the contrary, the dangers of AIDS are often invented by the homophobic imagination and, despite scientific and medical evidence opposing these dangers, remain virtually permanent.[4] And the dangers which are artificially constructed around AIDS appear to attach themselves to dangers that are perceived to exist in homosexuality. Because of this connection, efforts at education become exercises in repulsion and disgust, and many individuals plainly reject or resist information in favor of sustaining a fear of AIDS that is propelled by either ignorance or emotion.

The homophobic attitude develops a dependency on ideas and concepts which are factually untrue.[5] Following a process of socialization (which is partly historical), many of these negative ideas about homosexuality come to bear on AIDS. Homophobic attitudes are difficult to dismantle because of their eventual entrenchment in human fear[6] that is successfully socialized and intrinsic to cultural attitudes in general.

So clearly, homophobia is a significant factor in the alienation of homosexuality and persons who experience this is, that occurs directly in confrontation with AIDS. I want to suggest that a socially constructed homophobia in the context of AIDS rests on historical roots. Within traditional psychoanalytic approaches it might be possible to argue that this origin exists in a prehistoric trauma around a mythic episode and follows from a subsequent socialization of this event in terms of a male parent ideal, and there is sufficient material in Freud to develop this idea convincingly.[7] The evidence for this trend is discernible in many broad historical and clinical approaches as well.[8] But while this theme might merit some hypothetical attention, it remains well beyond the scope of this discussion. Nevertheless, it will be one of the aims of this paper to explore some of the ways theology and psychology construct meanings for AIDS in its primary association with a clearly homosexual epidemiology.

For religion in the West, homosexuality is unacceptable for reasons which have as their bases a fundamental and apparently irreducible theological justification.[9] Homosexuality is negated through historically and therefore culturally entrenched moral attitudes. A justification seems to exist somewhere deep within the western religious psyche for hatred and intolerance against the gay population. Antipathy toward gays seems to become ethical and seems to be encouraged by and through much Christian theology. It is not surprising, given a clearly anti-homosexual history of theology, that a distinct Christian ambivalence becomes increasingly clear in the context of AIDS.

But in assessing the meaning of AIDS from a psychological-functional perspective, another important question arises: is there not, possibly, some motivation existing beneath the theological rationale for despising homosexuality— some hidden psychological precipitate that provokes the alienation of homosexuality to begin with?

If we approach this question from an historical perspective we might ask whether some ancient event, now eroded from human recollection but still embedded deeply within the human imagination, is responsible for the way the contemporary Church regards homosexuality in the context of AIDS. While we have agreed not to develop this theme too exactly, an opportunity presents for approaching the Church's position on homosexuality in terms of its origins.

By separating the aims of the Church's position on homosexuality from the bases of these aims, we arrive at two more questions. What is the psychological function of the anti-homosexual position of the Christian church in terms of its aims and potential for gratification? Second, on what is it based in terms of original motivation and source? In other words, what original episode resulted in the perception of danger around homosexuality which leads, historically to the entrenchment of anti-gay sentiment in cultural systems? And to what end is an anti-gay theology directed?

The term "homophobia" refers to an intense and exaggerated fear of homosexuality as it is "perceived" to be a dangerous external thing. While itself constitutes some form of suffering, the term "homophobia" also causes suffering—it is "pathogenic" in the classic meaning.[10] Typically, when a homophobic individual is confronted directly with homosexuality, the reaction is one of fear, disgust, nausea, anxiety and, inevitably, judgment and defense. As a form of very

thorough rejection of homosexual experiences, a homophobic reaction has implications in a variety of psychosocial and
religious contexts, and influences AIDS in a manner which is
problematic. Inevitably, the perception of homophobic fear
by homosexuals and persons with AIDS alike contributes to
psychiatric, psychological and neurological (stress related)
complications.[11]

While the expression of homophobia is particularly ac-
centuated in the context of AIDS, it is not entirely because
of AIDS that this fear develops. Rather, AIDS provides a
space into which pre-existing fears of homosexuality organize, collaborate and become evident. Homophobia is not un-
common when homosexuality is apprehended through the
disease metaphor of AIDS. AIDS that seems to predicate
homosexuality with the same fatality that the early Church
conceived around Sodom: a form of human experience
connected with depravity and death.

It is tempting, furthermore, to theorize it is the Sodom
story which presents us with an original, traumatic event of
mythic proportions upon which all subsequent responses to
homosexuality within Western culture are structured. Equally, it is difficult, if not impossible, to disentangle the persistent relationship that seems to form between the Sodom story
and AIDS. Bailey suggests that the Sodom story was immediately accepted by the Christian Church, and

> *has remained authoritative and virtually un-
> changed until now teaching that those who in-
> dulge in unnatural vice may bring upon them-
> selves and upon all who tolerate their depravity
> the fearful vengeance of God. Together, the
> Bible and Sodom have exercised a powerful in-
> fluence upon the thought and the imagination of
> the West in the matter of homosexual prac-
> tices.*[23]

Popular Moral Majority leader Jerry Falwell, writing his commentary column for his *Liberty Report*, says: "AIDS is a lethal judgment of God on the sin of homosexuality and it is also the judgment of God on America for endorsing this vulgar, perverted and reprobate lifestyle."[13] And sustaining the ancient connection of homosexuality with its theological origins in Sodom, Falwell states further:

> *God says ... that homosexuality is a perverted and reprobate lifestyle. God also says those engaged in such homosexual acts will receive "in their own persons, due penalty of their error." God destroyed Sodom and Gomorrah primarily because of the sin of homosexuality. Today, He is again bringing judgment against this wicked practice through AIDS . . . homosexuals are gaining control of towns and communities . . . we must preserve America by convicting her of sin and the folly of endorsing a lifestyle that is strangling the very life out of her....*[14]

In *Sodomy and the Future of America*, P. J. Leithart extends the position that homosexuality is a grave danger to Christian American civilization because it trespasses normativity so blatantly: "The homosexual subculture and AIDS threatens, perhaps more profoundly than any other problem, the very survival, both physical and social, of the West and of America in particular."[15] Further, Leithart reveals the Christian concept of homosexuality as theological antithesis:

> *[H]omosexuality is the cultural culmination of rebellion against God. It represents the 'burning out' of man and his culture. This is true because the homosexual strikes at the very cornerstone of human society.... A homosexual culture is opposed at every point to Christianity. It must*

therefore be combatted with every available weapon .... Unless the Church takes up [its responsibilities against homosexuality] the West will continue its suicidal descent into barbarism.[16]

Specifically, it is probable the legalistic anti-homosexual position of the Church that is founded upon the Sodom story provides a central moral orientation for the socio-cultural suppression of homoeroticism in the West.

AIDS figures prominently for homophobia as a metaphor. The perils connected with homosexuality in the Sodom story (death results from gay sex) become literal, medical facts which tell the old story.

In the homophobic imagination, AIDS and homosexuality are equated with disease and death. In the case of Christianity, homosexuality is structured entirely in metaphors of moral antithesis[17] and becomes perennially symbolic of heresy, madness and estrangement. Gay sex is an act of ultimate disobedience to God. In gaining the predicates of moral antithesis for which punishment is likely, the suppression of homosexuality becomes a reasonable, survival-oriented choice (something one does, by necessity, to avoid the fatal punishment modelled in the Sodom story). When affiliated with a God, any social sanctions against homosexuality regain their original theological status, and punishment for gay sex is supported by the divine prerogative that is modelled in the Sodom story.

The implications for homosexual persons within the Christian tradition are self-evident. If homosexuality is dangerous and an individual is homosexual, then the homosexual person is also dangerous. Experiencing this to be true, one of the things homosexuals develop is an adaptational defense system to protect themselves from the conditions which would potentially harm them. But this does not occur in the primary sense that gay people become frightened of their own homoerotic orientations and appetites, nor are they afraid of the objects of their yearning. This would be exceptional since homosexuals, like their heterosexual counterparts like their erotic objects and are aroused by them. Rather, the defensive position unique to gay people perceives that culture and society are dangerous as a direct result of the homophobic manner in which homosexuality (a portion of self) is socially and culturally constructed. It is not surprising either that much psychiatric discourse on homosexuality is written in the clinical terminology of paranoia.[18]

Besides being socially constructed as a dangerous kind of experience, homosexuality may also be internally constructed as a "bad" kind of experience. This latter activity is related in psychiatric discourse to the preservation of an internal superego, the internalized parent or god who sanctions against homosexuality.[19] In a sense, the internal fear that is constructed around homosexuality is the personal counterpart of the external trend of homophobia which becomes socialized in morality, civil law and religion. Bakan tells us that the superego is frequently associated with a sense of threat, and calls it "a kind of gathering place for the death-instinct."[20]

I want to suggest that this internal form of prohibition responds directly to the theological God who becomes both visible and dangerous to the homosexual as a person. In a life characterized by suspicion and secrecy, the homosexual person may be pursued by punitive objects, and may even succumb to death by suicide in order to restore some sense of personal volition and control against the forces which exist against gay experience. A compensation for external social controls may develop in gay experience which clinically manifests as a need to empower oneself despite the consequences: the connection is often made between narcissism, homosexual panic and suicide.[21]

Death due to AIDS is something more or different than death by cancer or homicide. It objectifies the perceptions of fatality associated, for many reasons, with homosexuality and secondarily because of this connection, with alienation. It is, perhaps, "what happens" to homosexuals represented in an extreme form. Robert Cecchi of New York Gay Men's Health Crisis Center supports this idea in his theoretical *Stress Prodrome to Immune Deficiency*:

> *[I]mmune breakdown may be the result of stress associated with lack of positive self-image, inability to express feeling and anger, inability to complete relationships, loss of family, lack of community nurturance, lack of supportive role models, and lack of self-acceptance and identity ... AIDS is an illness affecting many people who are in society's disfavor, people cast out and rejected for their differences.*[22]

If, in fact, Christian theology bases its fundamental anti-homosexual disposition on homophobic precipitates, then is such a process not itself pathological, *viz.* symptomatic of a more basic problematic condition which remains otherwise intentionally concealed? Does a theology which perpetuates hostility against homosexuality reveal a kind of morbid fear of gay sex that is normally concealed within ethics or morality or even theology itself? Is the expression of morbid fear and dread by theology toward homosexuality not itself constructed around something similar to homosexual panic? Does AIDS awaken a neurosis embedded within Christian theology? Does homophobia, founded on the trauma of Sodom betray "pathological" origins within the history of theology, in particular around its preoccupation with the Sodom story?

The God represented by Christian theological tradition, in which these sanctions gain considerable power, has not been congenial to the homosexual throughout perhaps a thousand years of human history. In the beginning,

the Church taught and people universally be-
lieved ... that homosexual practices had brought
a terrible Divine vengeance upon ... Sodom, and
that the repetition of such offenses against
nature had from time to time provoked similar
visitations in the form of earthquake and famine
... [that] steps should be taken to ward off the
wrath of God which might be displayed against
the filii diffidentiae:[23]

It is most acutely through AIDS that we gain an immediate and potentially frightening picture of the church's contemporary understanding of homosexuality as this understanding reflects and reiterates an ancient historical position.
So psychologically entrenched are the negative attitudes toward homosexuality that they appear to exist as a type of
biological and thereby wholly natural way of thinking. Yet,
under cautious scrutiny, they cannot be considered natural.
First, beyond the parallels made with the Sodom story, the
typical Christian position on homosexuality in the context
of AIDS reflects a particular understanding of sexuality. Sexuality in the West has been very distinctly separated from all
other forms of experience for some time.

Within the Western Christian tradition, a model of heterosexuality functions as a paradigm of obedient cooperation
with a theological entity who himself prefers matrimonial
models that can produce offspring. Foucault provides an example of this idea when he writes of the nineteenth century:

Sexuality was carefully confined; it moved into
the home. The conjugal family took custody of
it and absorbed it into the serious function of re-
production. On the subject of sex, silence be-
came the rule. The legitimate and procreative
couple laid down the law ... [and] imposed it-
self as model, enforced the norm, safeguarded

the truth.[24]

God is represented throughout Christianity as favoring
heterosexual experience over homosexual experience even to
the point of sanctifying heterosexual relations and building a
meaning for homosexuality that is unholy, illegitimate and
disgusting, etc. Still, any models of heterosexuality within
the Christian tradition are void of pleasure. Rather, the focus
of Christian models of sexuality is upon procreation--pro-
geny. Homosexual love is not sanctified like matrimony since
homosexuals do not among themselves produce offspring;
homosexuality has always represented to Christianity a kind
of sexuality that is—differently than heterosexuality—perceived to be consumed only with pleasure, lust and egoism.

In turning away from the act of procreation (heterosexual coitus) homosexuality came to represent the opposite of
progeny: death and an outward defiance of life. To deviate
from the model of procreative sexuality meant that one did
also turn from God. This placed the homosexual person in
jeopardy. For these reasons, and for some others, the homosexual has always been afraid to face this God as a whole
person.[25]

Secondly, AIDS provides the pre-existing Christian position on homosexuality: a space in which to grow which
reiterates ancient tendencies to regard homosexuality as a
condition which causes plague. With the epidemiology of
AIDS, homosexuality is attached to a radically publicized
terminal disease. Plague, as a punitive expression of divinity
in the created world is the result of God's intervention in the
realm of the immoral vicissitudes of humankind.

In this idea the perils of homosexuality truly begin to
gain ground. Consistent with the plague metaphor, AIDS
defies medical efficacy so openly: "It [awakens] the age-old
fear that medicine is powerless in the face of a new disease,
the fear of suffering and the fear of death."[26]

The resistance on the part of AIDS to a favorable reduc-

tion of morbidity despite all medical efforts leads to a kind
of apocalyptic neurosis in the popular Western imagination.
This neurosis consists of phobic, hysterical and paranoid
trends which themselves are nurtured where homosexuality
and AIDS mingle under the same original tree of perversion
and dread. AIDS became almost immediately an epidemic
thus lending certain smallness to even the most sophisticated
scientific endeavors. The failure of human power toward cure
results in a quick association, because of the sheer scale of
AIDS, with prior manifestations of disease that were usually
divinely-motivated and beyond human control. How else
could something so awful occur, if it did not come from
some place wholly removed from human interaction, from
God? Why, in fact, would such a disease take hold of homosexuals to begin with?

If it were merely the result of human interaction, then
logically human efforts would succeed in developing tech-
niques to mitigate the fatality of AIDS. The existential turmoil and frustration resulting from the difficult problems
around the control of AIDS led to assigning the disease
some divine attributes, thereby both exchanging human responsibility with divine will while at the same time adding
substantially to a complexification of AIDS.

For some, the consequences of homosexuality are so
severe as to provoke equally severe and uncompromising
punishments. Once more God is predicated with values which
pre facto despise homosexuality to such an extent that its
rumored obliteration through AIDS becomes fused with a
series of historical precedents. This is, after all, what occurred
at Sodom, and as many writers have suggested, since. This is
problematic for me since AIDS is not a plague. Moral values
cannot rest upon microscopic physiopathogens. If for Christianity the deaths of thousands of homosexuals is similar to
the fall of Sodom, it reveals one of the ways homosexuality is
perceived by the Christian imagination to constitute jeopardy
—not only for the homosexual, but for the created world in

which they live. It betrays, in fact, a homophobic disposition.

Taken in this light, homosexuality is conceived as a wholly illegitimate expression of human experience, as antithetical and thereby deserving of God's wrath in the form of modern punitive plague. Beyond this, however, one may interpret the religious use of plague in reference to AIDS to mean that homosexuals, in inviting plague, deserve to die because what and who they are offends a larger metaphysical plan. Otherwise, why would AIDS exist at all if not to rid the world of homosexuality, moral corruption and sin? The world therefore is protected by God through the extinction of homosexuality through AIDS. The formation of this kind of rationale is entirely tautological.

Third, this trend in thinking creates another pathological space within the Christian Church for and because of homosexuality. The homosexual who exists within this space experiences a reverberating sense of alienation both from the community and from the God who is apprehended by this collective appeal to morality. When AIDS is conceived of as plague, then homosexuality constitutes one example of the immoral vicissitudes of humankind that invites punishment from a metaphysical creator: God turns against homosexuals with a fearful vengeance.

The corollary is exceptionally simple. This means that homosexuals are illegitimate persons since they oppose a created purpose or divine ideal as this is upheld and taught in the Christian context. This represents not only modes of thinking and cognition, but visceral, phenomenological reality—a very problematic ontological sense of being for gay individuals. Homosexual people then face being wiped out by the metaphysical entity whose existence they oppose through their sexual behavior or—and this is not the rule but rather the Christian ideal—the sexual behavior changes to accommodate the divine imperatives regarding sexuality.

The transformation of the homosexual into a sanctified created being can only occur if homosexuality itself is regarded, according to salvific ideas, as sin (*i.e.*, denied and forgotten). In this manner, homosexuality must become charged with guilt. However, one might potentially avoid plague if one changes something toward which the divine punitive intervention is aimed. An example of this can be seen in *Perhaps Today* magazine under a headline in the "Letters We Love" column which claims: "Man rescued from homosexuality through AIDS telecast."[27] There have been numerous examples of homosexual men with AIDS who have repented of their homosexuality in the hope that God will relieve them of the homosexual disease. The conscious suppression leads to human anguish since the denial of one's sexuality is, if nothing else, an impoverishment of the whole person whose desires for intimacy still aim for satisfaction.

The intrinsic alienation of homosexuality thus becomes the alienation of homosexual persons, the alienation becomes a normative portion of experience for those who share, whether by choice or inheritance, a Christian heritage combined with homosexual experience. The conflict between the two is a source of crippling anxiety and psychological confusion which readily comes to bear on the meaning of AIDS for the twentieth century. In other words, for many homosexuals, the call to salvation constitutes a form of existential peril and *dis*-ease. If AIDS is the plague which affects homosexuals, then it seems to provide the space for Christianity to theologize their alienation, their outrageous separation from others for whom the plague is perceived to present no peril. This idea extends from the moral atmosphere surrounding sexuality and carries homosexuality into the disease metaphor that encompasses AIDS as a plague.

But even without the disease metaphor which supports the theological position on homosexuality, this form of sexual expression had been predicated as madness, heresy or simply sin: it was already illegitimate before AIDS came along. Thompson calls homosexuality "a wastebasket to which all friendly and hostile feelings toward members of one's sex are applied." [28] AIDS merely permits a space into which this projection of illegitimacy coupled with peril may grow stronger and more comprehensive.

So rather than experiencing a theology of freedom, liberation and salvation, homosexuals within the Christian context have been driven into deception, suppression and perennial anguish. They are warned against their natural inclinations through the threat of divine plague, of mortal, mysterious extinction. If homosexuals themselves experience alienation due to a theology which serves as a warning, it is only in their own best interest that they in turn alienate that portion of selfness for which this alienation exists. Once this is accomplished they may approximate the moral paradigms which comprise Christian conscience (*i.e.* marriage or celibacy). This is not a complicated process either. The theological perception historically connects conscious volition with homosexuality: homosexuals *choose* their sexual proentation. [29] Simply, if homosexuals want to co-exist with the moral and theological position that is typical of the Christian Church, they cannot be homosexuals (*viz.*, themselves). They must choose to be something else, and they can do this by first renouncing the homosexual part of themselves as sin and moving along with their new transformed Christian lives leave sin behind them.

As Bakan suggested, something perceived as pain or disease or sin is estranged from an otherwise sense of wellbeing. The perception of pain creates a sense of telic decentralization, of dis-ease within one's self. The "bad things" are differentiated from the whole person, cast off, projected into pathological entities, into "not me" objects. These objects are perceived as "burdens" which must be carried around unless some relief can be found. [30] This means that a preponderance of suppression must be functional which forces homosexuality, as a portion of the self, into the unconscious, into "not me" objects. The idea that one can be fragmented into "good" and "bad" parts is a very difficult and dangerous one for homosexuals. Yes, if we apply this model to the Church, we can see a similar pattern of fragmentation and estrangement constructed in models of salvation.

If homosexuality is conceived by Christianity to constitute a disease, heresy, madness, etc., this occurs only in the interest of differentiating the truly "bad" things from the "good" ones; in other words, for separating moral from immoral. But as mentioned earlier, this is more than just *theo*-logy, words and ideas spoken in the name of God. It becomes a portion of experience for both those who cast off the bad objects as well as for those individuals who, in fact, "are" cast off as inherently evil. What occurs is that homosexuality within the Christian tradition is not only identified with a whole series of negative predicates, and thus considered to be a "burden" requiring relief or redemption, but also identifies with these values as far as they are believed and experienced.

AIDS, continuous with the pre-existing association of homosexuality with plague and divine prerogative (Sodom), supports the alienation of homosexuality in a way which is literal and far less metaphorical or ideological than mere "heresy": it "proves" the legitimacy of the standard moral position which believes that homosexuality leads to death because it succeeds at offending God so greatly. *Christian Crusade* carried the headline "Scourge of AIDS serves its purpose."[31] *The Sword of the Lord* asks, "The pestilence of AIDS—is it the Judgment of God?"[32] "AIDS: A revelation of the righteous wrath of God," announces *The Standard Bearer*.[33]

In sustaining the "literalization" of the disease metaphor, it becomes necessary to ask about "who is to blame" in equally literal terms. This developed around the theoretical origins of HIV in African green monkeys and sheep. Soon, the mediaeval connection between homosexuality and bestiality re-appeared, when the original African virus was conceived to have survived the transition from the animal to the human host because of apparent homosexual depravity.[34] I have yet to uncover this suggestion in any of the clinical literature, yet it remains embedded in the popular imagination that AIDS began with bestiality. Because of the threat of epidemic, the pre-existing associations of homosexuality with bestiality and death, some "one" or "thing" must assume the blame and accept the culpability for bringing death to the world through perversion. And due to the homosexual epidemiology of AIDS established close to its discovery in 1981, this culpability falls directly upon the gay population in the West.

Without imperatives established against homosexuality by Christianity the meaning of AIDS as plague would vanish and there would be no reason for plagues to exist against gay people. This type of theology creates, largely for reasons which fall apart under ethical and moral scrutiny a type of "sexual apartheid" which previously had been reserved for women. Homosexuals are separated and driven away from the normative spaces by virtue of their sin, yet even when they exist outside the ecclesiastical boundaries where they belong they sustain illegitimacy and invite plague. A theology which arbitrarily but for apparently historical or metaphysical reasons alienates homosexuality and hence homosexual persons also creates within its own boundaries or community a pathological space for these individuals where survival is a perilous episode of avoidance and prohibition. They may relate to this theology only in the activity of denying some portion of their own created self-ness. This means, of course, that the denial of homosexuality is implicit in the assimilation and accommodation of any kind of theology whose salvific imperatives first consider homoerotic love a moral evil, and second require that it is therefore renounced as such if salvation is to be successful. Gay people must give up something in order to achieve the freedom promised by this same theology. But this giving-up activity frequently implies that some portion of the self is imprisoned in the tasks of repression and suppression. One turns not toward life, acceptance and a benevolent enternity, but away from the self through denial toward death, despair and darkness. One by necessity "hides" from the God who despises. This action is not absurd but essential in the struggle for human value, and this turning away itself constitutes some form of activity which is important and worth looking into. It implies the urgency for a kind of reinvention of a religion which is uncondiioned, relevant and real, unopposed to those things which put the homosexual at risk within the walls of the usual spaces of Church and holiness.

Given the context of theological discourse in Western culture, death due to AIDS might exist for gay people as a symbol of liberation from the experience of illegitimacy and alienation. It might elevate AIDS to a level of metaphysical significance: the homosexual who dies of AIDS is sometimes regarded as a martyr, and this metaphor is a popular one. Death is paradoxically meaningful for both the person with AIDS and while fully punitive and conceived in terms of vengeance wholly rational for those looking on for whom homosexuality represents the antithesis of created purpose and the direction of nature. AIDS as plague extinguishes the homosexual in a way which is uniquely religious (in a sense *poetic*) and thereby satisfactory, and this view might be shared by both modern Christians and by homosexuals who by inheritance or by virtue of their early developmental experience share the same theological god who despises them not for what they do but for who they actually are.

A demonstrative and thereby "real" guilt factor has been shown to provide significant variability in both the AIDS prodrome and throughout prognosis.[35] Guilt is a religious thing the churches could do something with that might be positive, forgiving and eventually reciprocal. They could absolve homosexuality of its moral and punitive stigma, relieve it of its heretical predicates, and thereby relieve human individuals of anguish and moral jeopardy through a new form of comprehensive salvation. They could do away with guilt for the AIDS prognosis and this medical fact might undergo some changes. This has been scientifically demonstrated to be of significance in the production and maintenance of T-helper cells and levels of immunity. But, the will of God as it is understood by the community whose god it is, would be compromised. If this is the God whom we fear, then we will hardly find it a simple thing to bolster individual empowerment in an effort to contradict the ancient admonition regarding the depravities of homosexuality. Fear thus prevents any positive changes and maintains and perpetuates the longevity of the historical position even further.

In discussing a Christian response to AIDS, I have implied that there is first a pathological space which motivates a religious alienation of homosexuality historically, and following this model, suggest further that this "original cause" exists as a point of reference for the Church and indeed Western society in general with regard to homosexuality. I have hinted that Sodom functions in the Christian imagination as this original trauma. Second, religion creates and sustains a pathological space for individuals whom some portion of homosexuality presents by making its renunciation a requisite for salvation. Third, there is a pathological space which envelops homosexuality through the metaphor that AIDS is a plague since homosexuality is, for these other two reasons, very, very wrong. Clearly, the whole process is built on premises of deception and misconception, yet resists any favorable transformations due to an overarching presence of fear.

Finally, a corollary presents that if Christianity alienates homosexuality due in part to an inherent obedience to a patriarchal deity who despises homosexuality for ancient reasons, and this is particularly pronounced within the metaphorical contest of AIDS as plague, then homosexuality equally alienates Christianity in the same context because this deity is just plain alienating and unacceptable over a period of a lifetime. In rejecting the homosexual first for metaphysical and historical reasons then later because of the plague of AIDS through which divine displeasure becomes apparent, the Church gives accidental birth to a new form of compensatory theology. In fulfilling the promise of the "fearful vengeance of God," AIDS then writes its own theology of alienation to which the homosexual, the outcast and the sinner subscribe.

In compensating for alienation, the homosexual on the outside of Christianity reformulates religion in order to face a God who is together accepting of the self as a whole person in a way which is loving, lasting and meaningful. The perceived contagion of AIDS results in taboos which forbid human touch due to a fear of contagious death. But for those directly affected by AIDS, human touch has become the new logos. Human touch provides reasonable consolation that, as a created human being, some essential things of like—like self and sexuality—are at least as "good" as they are important. This rebellious act, in reaching through alienation, disease and despair, truly recognizes that God is love.

—Bruce L. Mills

NOTES

[1] R. L. Blaney & G. E. Piccola, "Psychologic issues related to AIDS," *Journal of the Medical Association of Georgia* 76 (1987), pp. 28-32; P. Chodoff, "Fear of AIDS," *Psychiatry* 50 (1987), pp. 184-191; M. E. Faulstich, "Psychiatric aspects of AIDS," *American Journal of Psychiatry* 144 (1987), pp. 551-556; D. Miller, "HIV-counseling: Some practical problems and issues," *Journal of the Royal Society of Medicine* 80 (1987), pp. 278-281.

[2] D. Altman, *Homosexual Oppression and Liberation* (London: Allen Lane, 1971); J. Hart & D. Richardson, *The*

Theory and Practice of Homosexuality (London: Routledge and Kegan Paul, 1981); C. W. Socarides, *The Overt Homosexual* (New York: Grune and Stratton, 1968).

[3] M. Gold, N. Seymour & J. Sahl, "Counselling HIV Seropositives," in L. McKusick (ed.), *What to do About AIDS: Physicians and Mental Health Professionals Discuss the Issues* (Berkeley: University of California Press, 1986), pp. 103-110; Health and Welfare Canada/Santé et Bien-être Canada, *The Report of the Expert Working Group on Integrated Palliative Care for Persons With AIDS* (draft), (Ottawa, Ontario: Federal Centre for AIDS, 1986).

[4] D. Scanlan, "Homophobia," *Ottawa Citizen* (10 November 1986), D-1 / D-3; 1986; E. V. Valdiserri, "Fear of AIDS: Implications for mental health practice with reference to egodystonic homosexuality," *American Journal of Orthopsychiatry* 56 (1985), pp. 634-638.

[5] I. M. Marks, *Fears and Phobias* (New York: Academic Press, 1969), J. C. Nemiah, "Psychoneurotic disorders," in A. M. Nicholi, Jr. (ed.), *The Harvard Guide to Modern Psychiatry* (Cambridge, MA: Belknap Press, 1978).

[6] W. S. Agras, D. Sylvester, and D. Oliveau, "The epidemiology of common fears and phobia," *Comprehensive Psychiatry* 10 (1969), pp. 151-156.6.

[7] S. Freud, *The Pelican Freud Library* [14 vols.] Angela Richards (ed.), 1973-1982; Albert Dickson (ed.) (Harmondsworth, Middlesex [UK] : Penguin, 1982-1985):
1905. Three essays on the theory of sexuality. *On Sexuality* Vol. 7.
1906. My views on the part played by sexuality in the aetiology of the neuroses. *On Psychopathology*. Vol. 10.
1907. Obsessive actions and religious practices. *The Origins*

of Religion. Vol. 13.

1911. Psychoanalytic notes on an autobiographical account of a case of paranoia (*Dementia Paranoides*) (Schreber). *Case Histories II.* Vol. 9.

1913. Totem and taboo. *The Origins of Religion.* Vol. 13.

1927. The future of an illusion. *Civilization, Society and Religion.* Vol. 12.

1930. Civilization and its discontents. *Civilization, Society and Religion.* Vol. 12.

[8] C. R. Badcock, *The Psychoanalysis of Culture* (Oxford: Basil, 1980), D. S. Bailey, *Homosexuality and the Western Christian Tradition* (London: Longmans, Green, 1955); J. Boswell, *Christianity, Social Tolerance and Homosexuality* (Chicago: University of Chicago Press, 1980); T. Vangaard, *Phallos: A Symbol and its History in the Male World* (London. Jonathan Cape, 1969).

[9] J. McNeill, *The Church and the Homosexual* (Kansas City, MO: Sheed, Andrews and McMeel, 1976).

[10] K. Schneider, *Clinical Psychopathology* (London: Grune and Stratton, 1959).

[11] R. Cecchi, "Stress prodrome to immune deficiency," in I. J. Selikoff, A. S. Teirstein and S. Z. Hirschman (eds.), *Acquired Immune Deficiency Syndrome* (Annals of the New York Academy of Sciences, Vol. 437; New York: The New York Academy of Sciences, 1984), pp. 286, 289.

[12] Bailey, *op. cit.*, pp. 153, 154.

[13] J. Falwell, "AIDS: The judgment of God," *Liberty Report* 2 (April 1987), pp. 2, 5.

[14] *Ibid.*

[15] P. L. Leithart, "Sodomy and the future of America," *The Biblical World View* (February 1988), pp. 7-8.

[16] *Ibid.*

[17] C. Bingham, "Seventeenth century attitudes toward deviant sex," *Journal of Interdisciplinary History* 1 (1971), pp. 463-465; M. Goodich, *The Unmentionable Vice: Homosexuality in the Later Medieval Period* (Santa Barbara, CA: ABC-CLIO, 1979).

[18] S. Ferenczi, "Types of Males Homosexuality," trans. E. Jones, in C. Berg and A. M. Krich (eds.), *Homosexuality: A Subjective and Objective Investigation* (London: Allen and Unwin, 1958), pp. 227-242.

[19] I. Bieber, H. J. Dain, P. R. Dince, *et al.*, "Homosexuality: A psychoanalytic study of male homosexuals," *Psychiatry* 18 (1955), pp. 163-173.

[20] D. Bakan, *Disease, Pain and Sacrifice* (Chicago: University of Chicago Press, 1968), p. 43.

[21] H. Gershman, "Reflections on the nature of homosexuality," *American Journal of Psychoanalysis* 26 (1966), pp. 46-48, C. Watson, "A test of the relationship between repressed homosexuality and paranoid mechanisms," *Journal of Clinical Psychology* 21 (1965), pp. 380-384.

[22] Cecchi, *op. cit.*, pp. 286, 287.

[23] Bailey, *op. cit.*, p. ix.

[24] M. Foucault, *The History of Sexuality* (Vol. 1: An Introduction), trans. R. Hurley (New York: Vintage Books, 1980), p. 3.

[25] Boswell, *loc. cit.*

[26] Health & Welfare, Canada, *op. cit.*, p. 1.

[27] *Perhaps Today* (January/February 1988), p. 16.

[28] C. Thompson, "Changing concepts in psychoanalysis," in C. Berg and A. M. Krich, *op. cit.*, pp. 301-313.

[29] J. F. Harvey, *The Homosexual Person* (San Francisco: Ignatius Press, 1987).

[30] Bakan, *loc. cit.*

[31] *Christian Crusade* 34 (1987), p. 6.

[32] H. Pyle, "The pestilence of AIDS—Is it the Judgment of God?" *The Sword of the Lord* (November 15, 1985), p. 3.

[33] R. Cammenga, "AIDS: A revelation of the righteous wrath of God," *The Standard Bearer* (February 15, 1984), p. 207.

[34] J. Van Impe, *AIDS 150 Million by 1991* (Royal Oak, MI: Jack Van Impe Ministries, 1987), p. 29.

[35] Cecchi, *op. cit.*, p. 286.

CONCLUSION—
BEYOND HOMOPHOBIA
THROUGH COMING OUT

"Homophobia should not have the last word in a study whose ultimate goal is liberation. . . The discovery of socio-political empowerment, and of spiritual balance and psycho-physical wholeness, points toward the work and the pleasures, the tears of struggle and the tears of joy, which lie ahead."

"Coming Out":
Discovering Empowerment, Balance, and Wholeness

Those of us who are gay men or lesbians have begun to realize that theological reflection and praxis ultimately conflate for us: We are responsible for seeking, demanding, and creating justice and liberation. Conversely, our failures to assume responsibility, our fearful refusal to claim and to use our power, not only function to forestall our liberation: such failures and refusals may actually undercut out very humanity. Speaking for both women and gay people, for example, Carter Heyward contends that the "greatest sin" of an oppressed and marginalized people "has always been our failure to take ourselves seriously as strong, powerful, autonomous and creative persons"; moreover, "our fear of our strength may be our undoing. And our learning to stand and speak up for ourselves may well be our salvation."[1] In other words, while we clearly have the capacity to claim and to assert our pwer and our full humanity, to create redemptive and liberating justice for ourselves and for others, we can still choose passivity and inactivity instead. Whenever we accept the heterosexist devaluation of ourselves as merely one-dimensional and purely sexual beings; whenever we pursue assimilation into the hierarchies of acceptability and power instead of pursuing structural change; whenever we believe government or institutionalized religion or the medical research system will altruisticially protect our best interests; and, whenever we fail to participate in celebrations of gay pride or demonstrations for gay rights because someone else will "do it for us"—in all these instances do we abdicate our pwer. Such passive inactivity always shifts the responsibility for our liberation onto others. Moreover, as long as we do so, we willfully forfeit our full humanity as gay people before the forces of oppression.

The obvious alternative to such passive forfeiture of

either our full humanity or our liberation as gay men and lesbians is for us to (re)claim our power, our traditional/historical strength, and our in-born, created goodness. We can (re)-claim what has been within us all along, including not only our value and worth, but our capacities to effect change as well. Judaism provides the best historical example, within our western religious heritage, of both the refusal to accept powerlessness and the consequent empowerment of active and assertive endurance. The collective Jewish experience, as a frequently threatened and oppressed people, has developed a moral obligation not to encourage oppressors with passivity, but to eschew martyrdom by an assumption of protest and action against human injustice. Speaking from the historical standpoint of accumulated antisemitism and virtual genocide, Emil Fackenheim writes that "the voice of Auschwitz commands Jews . . . to accept their singled out condition, face up to its contradictions, and endure them. Moreover, it gives the power of endurance . . . . The Jews of today *can* endure because he [*sic.*] *must* endure, and he [*sic.*]must endure because he [*sic.*] is *commanded* to endure."[2] He subsequently describes a number of duties, the fulfillment of which empowers the oppressed, duties (1) to remember and to tell about persecutions, (2) to survive rather than to seek or to accept martyrdom, (3) to refuse either cynicism or otherworldliness, and (4) to continue to wrestle with God and to bear a kinship with all other victims of oppression.[3]

In other words, then, Jews are commanded to persevere, to sustain the continuum from past to future, by living fully in the present, by embodying the divine covenant with all marginalized people, and by empathetically sharing the agony and even death suffered by those who are different. At the same time, remembering God's demand for human justice, when coupled with the memory of the Holocaust, empowers ongoing Jewish efforts for justice, efforts to create hope and to (re)create God's presence in just human relationships. For gay men and lesbians, Jewish experience can be paradigmatic for our (re)discovering not only God's presence in suffering (whether in the anti-gay genocide in our own history, or in current homophobic violence, or in the tragedy of AIDS), but God's demand for justice as well. Much like for the Jews, our gay survival throughout history, our adamant refusal before anti-gay violence and politics to simply "go away," our refusal before AIDS to quit loving one another— in fact our loving each other even more deeply— and our persistent presence and visibility, are together the very sources of our power, of our capacity to act and to effect our liberation.

As conservative politics and religion have exploited the AIDS crisis to feed an already increasing homophobia, this demand that we claim and use our power has in turn become even more persistent. As the half-million participants in the October 1987 March on Washington for Lesbian and Gay Rights made clear, the time is past for wasting our energies in gay self-justification and in gay apologetics; the time is past for arguing over scripture and seeking assimilation into established churches and synagogues or into the clergy on "their" terms; and, the time is certainly past for passive inactivity, whether in regard to the sociopolitical or the religious realms. We must, instead, take up the tasks of forthrightly doing a gay theology-as-praxis, absolutely and without apology. We must take up the tasks of our own liberation, all of us, together. As Carter Heyward has said, "The time has come . . . to channel our . . . energies into the active realization of our power . . . and to make no apologies for being who and what we are"; in fact, "to become oneself is the only truly responsible way to be."[4] We must claim and use our power to effect liberation; and claiming our power means we must first (re)claim and (re)affirm ourselves. Only in claiming ourselves, in coming out, do we really begin to glimpse the immense power we actually have.

(i) Coming Out to Empowerment

Matthew Fox has described the "sacrament of 'coming

out' " as a "kind of letting go: a letting go of the images of
personhood, sexuality, and selfhood that society has put on
one in favor of trusting oneself enough to let oneself be oneself."[5] Those powerful images of heterosexist enculturation,
however, are very strong ones which often make coming out
a difficult process of anger and mourning over estranged familial relationships and lost professional possibilities, a process
of grieving for what life "might have been" otherwise, a process of often painful spiritual deepening and "letting go" in
order to accept and to affirm one's gay identity and to embrace one's exile on the margins of sociocultural acceptability.[6] Moreover, those of us determined to create a gay liberation theology, as well as those of us equally determined to
nurture the ongoing pursuit and creation of gay liberation,
face a double bind. We must advocate and nurture compassion, without condescension, for those numerous individuals
who feel that pressures of whatever sort warrant keeping the
closet door closed for now, while at the same time we must
insist that coming out *en masse* is both the only sure route to
authentic living as gay men and lesbians and the best means
for discovering and claiming our collective power to seek our
own liberation.

Albeit a process without the benefit(s) of culturally ritu-
alized support (or "rites of passage"), coming out is nevertheless a vitally important process of discovering and constructing an authentic self-identity "from within," of discovering
one's own truths, and thus of building "ontological security"
upon one's "own myths."[7] As such, coming out requires pen-
etrating one's depths, discovering one's center of meaning,
being, identity, and values, and beginning to live from this
newfound center or grounding as one's spiritual empowerment. The process may also include confronting and resolving
opposites, discovering the genuine balances or androgyny of
the unit-in-plurality of God/cosmos, and imploding the patri-
archally enculturated divisiveness of the self, thereby pene-
trating, confusing, and reconciling the opposites. For a gay

man, in particular, these aspects of the coming out process require a commitment to "ending male dominance *within himself."*[8]

For any individual, then, the deepening required by coming out, the process of discovering and constructing an authentic and centered self, can yield an "infinite enspiriting
empowering source," or grounding, for being gay in a homophobic society.[9] That process and its individual empowerment can further enable an individual to join with other gay
men and lesbians in community. In other words, coming out
exchanges the isolation of the closet for the nurturance of
community, whereby the empowerment of the freed and
centered self can be endlessly multiplied and further nourished for our joint efforts at liberation. Coming out, according
to Carter Heyward, then not only functions to free the individual from the closet, but on its communal side, also functions "to name social reality and to participate in its re-
imaging. It is to lift up for reassessment a piece of covert
public policy which needs overt public attention."[10] Coming
out is to move both toward claiming our responsibility for
right and just relationships and toward engaging in corrective
action. Coming out is, thus, not only an intensely personal
act, but a social, political, and spiritual act as well, as Heyward further elaborates:

> Coming out is a protest against social structures
> that are built on alienation between men and
> women, women and women, men and men.
> Coming out is the most radical, deeply personal
> and consciously political affirmation I can make
> on behalf of the possibilities of love and justice
> in the social order. Coming out is moving into
> relation with peers. It is not simply a way of
> being in bed, but rather a way of being in the
> world. . . . Coming out is an invitation to look
> and see and consider the value of mutuality in

196

> *in human life. Coming out is simultaneously a*
> *political movement and the mighty rush of*
> *God's spirit carrying us on.*[11]

Coming out moves us beyond isolation and "mere homosexual acts" to the realization of our gayness as an all-encompasing existential standpoint for being in the world, for nurturing community, for joining with God's empowering advocacy and companionship, and thus for effecting our liberation. Coming out is the way into our empowerment, as liberation-seeking and -creating people.

John Fortunato has been most astute to the ways in which coming out brings us to empowerment by first confronting us with the personal costs involved and with the realities of homophobia and anti-gay oppression. Only as we are able to deepen—to penetrate—our personal and collective experience(s) of oppression do we come through or come out to empowerment. He says that "being exiled puts us intimately in touch with our powerlessness [or our experiences of oppression] . . . . But precisely because we are confronted with the awareness, we [discover therein] spiritual empowerment," the empowerment required to act and to be.[12] Ironically for those of us indoctrinated to the "sinfulness" of anger, our personal anger experienced in grieving and later embracing our marginality, as well as our collective anger as a people embattled by homophobic oppression and even violence, can be an important resource for this empowerment. Rosemary Radford Ruether, for example, argues that our anger can be liberating and grace-filled insofar as it empowers us both to break from our socialization and to demand our liberation: "Only by experiencing one's anger and alienation can one move on, with real integrity, to another level of truth."[13] In other words, whenever we take responsibility for our lives and our liberation, genuine divinity is revealed as the empowerment and sustenance which can enable us to transcend self-pity and fear. We further discover divine empowerment as we realize the righteousness of our anger and the consequent need for prophetic, corrective action in the face of oppression. In fact, our anger at life's seeming unfairness (e.g.: AIDS), or at human injustice and cruelty is not opposed to God; it is actually nurtured by the divine presence on our behalf. Carter Heyward similarly describes God as an "indignant" or angry power against injustice and asserts that "without our crying, our yearning, our raging, there is no God."[14]   Our righteous and divinely nourished anger further enables us to transcend self-doubt, depression and madness, and to develop self-esteem and gay pride instead, virtues without which we can have no sense of self or of community.

Our anger alone, however, is not itself liberating, unless we are able to deepen and to temper our anger with a compassion equally borne of our experiences of oppression and of God-with-us therein. George Edwards contends, for example, that insofar as gay men and lesbians know human oppression and hatred, we also have a capacity for knowing the depths of God's love, for discovering God's empowerment at the margins. Our gay and excluded sexuality itself can actually become the very source of our compassion: "Love, without becoming antisexual, is carried beyond the [narrow] perimeters or sexuality . . . into the total arena of the liberation struggle."[15]

Our anger, our capacity for compassion, our marginalized sexual loving, and God's absolute nearness with and for us-- all of these resources constitute our particular power as lesbians and gay men. As such, our communal spiritual power is very different from a patriarchically conceived, hierarchically structured power of domination and subordination. Our same-sex love at the margins is, instead, a balancing, horizontal, mutually relational force in opposition to vertically distributed power, a love energy which champions and empowers the powerless, and thus a socially democratic power.[16] Our power is horizontal, reciprocal, shared in common and within our marginalized community; our power simply awaits our collective realization, reclamation, and shared enactment to create significant liberational change. Our power is not something we can possess as a tool or as a weapon; it is rather an abstract quality of our liberation, not as a goal which can be achieved once and for all, but as a process or communal journey in which we simultaneously celebrate what we have already achieved, while we continue to struggle. Says Carter Heyward, "Our strength is our commitment to *do something* about what we have experienced, to celebrate the just and change the unjust. . . . Our strength is our commitment to *live* our values."[17]

Heyward also continually reconnects us to the reality that our power, our capacities to reclaim and enact our power in the sociopolitical and religious realms, does not and cannot depend upon anyone or anything other than ourselves. We alone are responsible for claiming or failing to claim our power. Not only is our power not vertically given; God in fact depends on us in order for God to empower us in turn. This utterly horizontal, mutual, and communal nature of our power as gay men and lesbians, a power interdependent with divine advocacy and companionship, also constitutes our "faithfulness" as gay people. Insofar as we are able to synthesize both our experience(s) of oppression, our individual and collective anger, and our deepened compassion, and are thereby able to shape, claim, and enact our power in the ongoing process and tasks of liberation, through all of this do we emerge as a faithful liberation community. Heyward thus describes a faithful people as a committed, participating, and empowered people, when she says that,

> . . . To be faithful . . . is to touch and be
> touched—whether physically or otherwise—with
> a depth and quality of tenderness that actually
> helps create life where there is death, comfort
> where there is despair. To be faithful in our sex-

ualities is to live a commitment to mutual, reciprocal relations between and among ourselves in which no one owns, possesses, dominates, or controls . . . but rather in which [we participate together in the tasks of liberation]. [18]

Over and over again are we reminded theologically of our responsibility for our own liberation. Our sources for a gay liberation theology insist and exemplify a demand that we refuse passive victimization and that we take up the tasks of liberation instead. We are commanded not only to endure, but to act, to come out, to claim our individual power and to nurture our communal power, as lesbians and gay men. As we confront the pain and losses of coming out, as well as the realities of anti-gay oppression, we discover in our anger and in our capacities for empathy and compassion a peculiar, divinely nourished power. Moreover, we discover that we can not only accept, but actually embrace and prefer our place at the margins. We find there that our particular sexuality is not only the source or cause of our ostracism; rather our gay sexuality is a blessing which enables mutuality and reciprocity, and which consequently nurtures our horizontal and shared power to effect liberation as a people faithful to our created goodness, to God's *a priori* acceptance of us, and to God's intimate presence with and for us. Coming out and reclaiming our power to demand, seek, and create liberation transcends the heterosexist devaluation of our sexuality and instead lifts up our sexual mutuality as *the* sacred source and grounding of our power, both as a liberation community and as a force to be reckoned with in theology.

(ii) Creating Gay Balance and Wholeness

Our gayness as an all-encompassing existential standpoint for being in the world entails not only the possibility for us to reconcile and reunite our bodiliness and our spirituality; it

also enables us to cut across, to destroy, confuse, and conflate, all polarities and dualistic hierarchies, and thus to stand
prophetically, symbolically, and actually over against the predominant mythic structures of the west. Our being gay allows
us to embrace and to embody androgyny in its broadest possible sense, not only by affirming that spiritual existence is
only possible through bodily and sexual existence, but by
balancing, compromising, and mediating extremes or opposites, as well; our gay spirituality is that in us which seeks
to uphold the middle ground between the demands of homophobic enculturation to the "real world" and the yearnings
of our deeper, more basic being, our "primal humanness."[19]
Ezekial Wright and Daniel Inesse have even argued that our
"true spiritual function" is to lead others also toward a
reunion of the opposites, while Malcolm Boyd has similarly
suggested that "perhaps the chief contribution gays can make
to the rest of society is in relation to the human search for
wholeness."[20] Spirituality, bodiliness, sexuality, and the
drive toward balance and wholeness are one, grounded in the
horizontality of God-with-us.

As gay men and lesbians, our standpoint between the
rigid poles of gender as well as our refusal of the roles and
sexuality of opposites together function to undermine all the
other dualisms which are fundamental to hierarchical heterosexism, and to evoke and create fundamental wholeness and
balance instead. Our efforts in gay liberation theology are
called thereby to join *all* liberation theologies in articulating
"a wholistic understanding of human beings—a unity between
matter and spirit, mind and body, will and emotion," and an
androgynous balance which affirms the goodness of creation
through both ecological and human justice.[21] Our balancing
act to create and sustain unity by holding opposites in a conciliatory tension is nowhere more plain than in our place between the gender and gender role polarities.

While Carter Heyward, for example, argues that our same-
sex relationships may just offer the best opportunities for

real mutuality apart from gender roles within our present heterosexist culture,[22] Gerre Goodman and coauthors have said that,

> . . . *gayness, on a personal level, has to do with commitment and energy as well as sex, and on a societal level, with breaking out of conditioned behavior and sex-role stereotyping. [In fact], to reduce gayness to a simple question of sexuality is to [homophobically] belittle its impact both on the individual and on society.*[23]

Similarly, John McNeill contends that gay people can significantly help in "leading the whole human family to a new and better understanding of interpersonal love between equals [in mutuality and friendship] . . . rather than the patriarchal role-playing of tradition."[24] In each of these sources, we again find that our balancing position between the gender and gender role opposites is both a possibility and a responsibility. McNeill further makes plain the prophetic or demanding aspect of our balancing place, especially for gay men: "The [gay male] community is *potentially* free from the psychological need to establish their male identity by means of violence, . . . [re]conditioned by their ability to accept and celebrate their sexuality" as the source of other passions.[25] Gay men are thus called to be models of a new masculinity free of both violence and domination, spiritually open and receptive instead, and to be both symbols and embodiments of a secure male identity *without* gender roles.

Ara Dostourian anticipates many of these concerns in his own earlier writing. Focusing upon the ways in which traditional gender-based roles of domination and subordination preclude genuine uncoercible love, he contends that gay men and lesbians already find the polarization of sex roles "false and destructive" and therefore reject those roles and instead affirm their humanity apart from the sanctification of either "acceptable" sexual preference or gender roles, thus repudiating the "domination-subordination syndrome."[26] Only overcoming or destroying the roles allows for equality, mutuality, and truly human relations. What ultimately comes through Dostourian's work is a call for gay men and lesbians to be at the forefront of a process which moves sexuality from the possessiveness of domination/subordination and gender roles toward mutually "intimate friendship, care and concern for others."[27] He thus describes and advocates a spectrum, rather than any hierarchy, by which to understand and (re)create relational forms and sexual expressions.

Fortunately, we actually have an historical precedent or model for the third-gender, intermediate, balancing function of our gay being, albeit a paradigm outside western, Judaeo-Christian culture. The native American berdaches may in fact be our best example of homosexual persons who were able, through interaction with one another, their cultures, and their communities, to synthesize both sexuality and spirituality, both masculinity and femininity, for both personal and social benefit, insofar as they consistently embodied a synthesis of spiritual and sexually different presence in their lives.[28] In his groundbreaking text,[29] Walter Williams describes the male berdache as a unique third gender intermediary between, and thus balancing, the opposites both of masculinity and femininity and of the psychic and the physical. Importantly, these individuals, who most frequently combined male and female attire with cross-gender occupations and homosexuality, were far from outcast by their precolonial native societies; they were instead a blessed and highly esteemed spiritual presence for their tribes, in accord with native mythology and religion. Williams describes native religion as believing that "the spirit of one thing (including a human being) is not superior to the spirit of any other"; such an egalitarian and ecological vision believes everything is spiritual.[30] Moreover, according to native religions, every human possibility exists for a reason, by divine intent, which provides a spiritual explanation for human difference, at once precluding exclusion and accepting human diversity—including the berdaches' role and sexuality. Says Williams,

> . . . Receiving instructions from a [spiritual] vision inhibits others from trying to change the berdache. . . . It also excuses the community from worrying about the cause of that person's difference, or the feeling that it is society's duty to try to change him. By the Indian view, someone who is different offers advantages to society precisely because she or he is freed from the restrictions of the usual.[31]

Among those advantages were that "native Americans, of course, saw no opposition between matters of the spirit and of the flesh."[32] The berdaches held together or balanced not only the spectrum of sexual and gender forces, but also the opposites of sacred (sky) and profane (earth), of clean and unclean, of mind and body, and of control and respect for nature. Moreover, the berdaches understood their sociocultural participation and the benefits they provided their tribes as part and parcel of their spirituality; as we would have our gay liberation theology, their theology and spirituality *was* their praxis.[33]

Williams is quick to point out, however, that the paradigmatic figure of the berdache is more androgynous, spiritual, and communally interconnected than urbanized and secular gay men, in particular, have tended to be. His work consequently admonishes gay men both to reclaim our spiritual aspects, our androgynous specialness, and our capacities for balancing sexuality and spirituality, and to embody a spectrum of sexual expressions and modes of being. He is especially concerned that gay men should focus, as did native cultures, upon individual character and the uniqueness of our gay perspective or sensibility, rather than upon mere sexual difference and sexual activity. Such skilled balancing, at our unique existential place on the margins of our cultural and religious traditions, may in fact be our special route to wholeness as gay people.[34]

Specifically now before the spectre of AIDS, John Fortunato has also emphasized the importance of our overcoming the fragmentation of our gay sexuality—from the wholeness of who we are—by a similar integration of our sexuality-spirituality-selfhood as the "inner cohesiveness" and grounding for confronting and transcending our experiences both of homophobic oppression and AIDS-related suffering.[35] As we are able to cease accepting and internalizing the homophobic devaluation of ourselves as fragmented and merely sexual people—which causes us to lose our good gay selves—and are able to openly assert our gay being and gay pride instead, then will we be equally able to move into a horizontal and intimate relation with a God who is "immanent, acting in the world, suffering with it and redeeming it through human agency."[36] As we are able to achieve such wholeness, we are also freed to realize that "concern for self must be balanced with steady social action"[37] and we are in turn empowered for the tasks of liberation: for combining prophetic outrage with out commitments both to social justice and to personal growth for *all* people, for doing justice in the face of contempt, and for "loving in the face of oppression."[38]

Ultimately, as we are able to come out and to accept and embrace our gay being and our gay selves as sanctified and good; as we are able to claim our power and capacity for achieving and creating social justice; as we are able to embody balance in our lives intimately interdependent with a God who stands with us as compassion and empowerment for justice-seeking and liberation—through all these marvelous activities do we discover, create, nourish, and sustain our wholeness as gay people. Moreover, upon the strength and power of our wholeness at the margins do we discover not only the blessing and love of divine presence, but our very ability to (re)envision and to build our gay community as truly that of a liberation people.

—J. Michael Clark, Ph.D.

NOTES

[1] I. Carter Heyward, *Our passion for justice: Images of power, sexuality, & liberation* (New York: Pilgrim Press, 1984), pp. 3, 131.

[2] Emil L. Fackenheim, *God's presence in history: Jewish affirmation & philosophical reflections* (New York: Harper & Row, 1970), p. 92.

[3] *Ibid.*, pp. 84-89.

[4] Heyward, *op. cit.*, pp. 3, 17.

[5] Matthew Fox, "The spiritual journey of the homosexual . . . & just about everyone else," in *A challenge to love: Gay & lesbian Catholics in the church*, ed. R. Nugent (New York: Crossroad/Continuum, 1983), p. 198.

[6] For a complete discussion of these and other related issues, see: John E. Fortunato, *Embracing the exile: Healing journeys of gay Christians* (New York: Seabury Press, 1983).

[7] Mitch Walker, *Visionary love: A spiritbook of gay mythology & transmutational faerie* (San Francisco: Treeroots Press, 1980), pp. 18-19.

[8] *Ibid.*, p. 88.

[9] *Ibid.*, p. 90.

[10] Heyward, *op. cit.*, p. 134.

[11] *Ibid.*, p. 82 (emphasis added).

[12] John E. Fortunato, *AIDS: The spiritual dilemma* (San Francisco: Harper & Row, 1987), p. 27.

[13] Rosemary Radford Ruether, *Sexism & God-talk: Toward a feminist theology* (Boston: Beacon Press, 1983), p. 188.

[14] I. Carter Heyward, *The redemption of God: A theology of mutual relation* (Washington, DC: University Press of America, 1982), pp. 55, 172.

[15] George R. Edwards, *Gay/lesbian liberation: A biblical perspective* (New York: Pilgrim Press, 1984), p. 125.

[16] Walker, *op. cit.*, pp. 23-25.

[17] Heyward, *Our passion for justice*, p. 128.

[18] *Ibid.*, p. 192.

[19] Ezekial Wright & Daniel Inesse, *God is gay: An evolutionary spiritual work* (San Francisco: Tayu Press, 1979), pp. 41, 43.

[20] *Ibid.*, p. 86; Malcolm Boyd, *Take off the masks* (Philadelphia: New Society Publishers, 1984), p. 167.

[21] Sheila D. Collins, "Feminist theology at the crossroads," *Christianity & Crisis* 41.20 (14 December 1981), p. 345.

[22] Heyward, *Our passion for justice*, pp. 81, 90.

[23] Gerre Goodman, **et al.**, *No turning back: Lesbian & gay liberation for the '80s* (Philadelphia: New Society Publishers, 1983), p. 15.

[24] John J. McNeill, S. J., "Homosexuality, lesbianism, & the future: The creative role of the gay community in building a more humane society," in *A challenge to love: Gay & lesbian Catholics in the church*, p. 55.

[25] *Ibid.*, p. 59 (emphasis added).

[26] Ara Doustourian, "Gayness: A radical Christian approach," in *The gay academic*, ed. L. Crew (Palm Springs: Etc. Publications, 1978), pp. 340, 341.

[27] *Ibid.*, p. 342.

[28] J. Michael Clark, *Gay being, divine presence: Essays in gay spirituality* (Garland, TX: Tangelwuld Press, 1987), pp. 28-47, especially p. 30.

[29] Walter L. Williams, *The spirit & the flesh: Sexual diversity in American Indian culture* (Boston: Beacon Press, 1986).

[30] *Ibid.*, p. 21.

[31] *Ibid.*, pp. 30, 42.

[32] *Ibid.*, p. 88.

[33] Clark, *op. cit.*, pp. 30, 33, 39, 43, 45.

[34] Williams, *op. cit.*, pp. 215-219.

[35] Fortunato, *AIDS: The spiritual dilemma*, p. 24.

[36] Collins, *op. cit.*, p. 347.

[37] Boyd, *op. cit.*, p. 167.

[38] Fortunato, *AIDS: The spiritual dilemma*, p. 32.

NOTES ON CONTRIBUTORS

J. MICHAEL CLARK (M.Div., Ph.D., Emory University) is currently co-chair of the Gay Men's Issues in Religion Group of the American Academy of Religion and is both an "independent scholar" and a part-time instructor in the Freshmen English Program of Georgia State University (Atlanta). He is the author of *A Place to Start: Toward an Unapologetic Gay Liberation Theology* (Dallas: Monument Press, 1989)—from which these two essays are excerpted--and *A Defiant Celebration: Theological Ethics and Gay Sexuality* (Garland, TX: Tangelwüld Press, 1990).

GARY DAVID COMSTOCK (M.Div., Bangor Theological Seminary, Ph.D., Union Theological Seminary) teaches philosophy and religion at Marist College (Poughkeepsie, NY) where he is also the Protestant chaplain. His areas of research in religious ethics include bias-related violence, gender and sexuality in Hebrew scripture, social justice for lesbians and gay men in contemporary society, and inclusive community building. His dissertation—from which this essay is excerpted—is scheduled for publication in book form by Columbia University Press during 1990.

LEWIS JOHN ERON (Ph.D., Temple University) is currently Associate Rabbi of Temple B'nai Abraham in Livingston, NJ. He has written a number of articles in the areas of Judaism in late antiquity and Jewish-Christian relations, and he is one of the co-authors of *The Jewish Jesus and the Christian Paul: Toward a New Foundation for Jewish-Christian Dialogue*, to be published by Orbis Press.

MARK R. KOWALEWSKI (Ph.D., School of Religion, University of Southern California) has published articles on gay men and AIDS, as well as on religious responses to the AIDS crises, He is currently a postdoctoral researcher with the Drug Abuse Research Group of UCLA.

BURCE L. MILLS (M.A., West Georgia College, M.A., University of Ottawa) is currently completing his Ph.D. in Religious Studies at the University of Ottawa, under Naomi Goldenberg, focusing on the influence of the Sodom story upon the contemporary meanings of AIDS. He facilitated two national conferences on AIDS in Canada (March 1990) and consults on appointment to the National Working Group on HIV infection and Mental Health of the Department of Health and Welfare of Canada.

CRAIG WESLEY PILANT (M.A., University of Illinois, M.S., Fordham University) is a Ph.D. candidate and teacher in historical theology at Fordham University.

MICHAEL L. STEMMELER (M. Theol., Eberhard-Karls University [Tübingen], M.A., Ph.D., Temple University) is currently co-chair of the Gay Men's Issues in Religion Group of the American Academy of Religion, and is an instructor in the Department of Religion and the Intellectual Heritage Program of Temple University.

THOMAS M. THURSTON (Ph.D., Graduate Theological Union, Berkeley) is currently negotiating for the publication of his recently completed text, *A Gay Liberation Theology*. An "independent scholar" in San Francisco, his current projects include "Natural Relations: A Response to Richard B. Hays' *Hermeneutics of Romans I*," and *Gay Weddings.*

INDEX

A statement from the publisher:

Freedom of communication is the indispensable condition of a healthy democracy. In a pluralistic society, it would be impossible for all people at all times to agree on the value of all ideas, and fatal to moral, artistic and intellectual growth if they did.

As the publisher of this important book, and as a participating member of the Consortium Publishers Associates, *we reject all barriers abridging access to any material, however controversial or even abhorrent to some. This press, and those united as* Publishers Associates, *are of the conviction that censorship of what any mortal sees or hears or reads constitutes an unacceptable dictatorship over our minds and a dangerous opening to religious, political, artistic, and intellectual repression.*

From 1982 to 1987, book banning has increased 107%. This is unacceptable. Imposing censorship protects only ignorance. It does the nation no good and harms the growth of the individual. Collectively and individually, the presses leagued as Publishers Associates *condemns the fascist tactics and totalitarian designs of such unAmerican groups as Beverly LeHaye's Concerned Women for America, Jerry Falwell's Liberty League (previously the Moral Majority [sic.]), and Don Wildemon's American Family Association. The First Amendment to the United States Constitution guarantees your right to read, see and hear whatever you choose.*

Read.